THE
INSTITUTIONAL
INVESTOR

SERIES IN FINANCE

International Corporate Finance

THE FINANCIAL MANAGEMENT ASSOCIATION SURVEY AND SYNTHESIS SERIES

This unique series provides corporate executives and professional investors with the practical tools vital for making sound financial decisions in today's competitive markets. Comprehensive and readable, each book in the series focuses on a relevant topic, integrating research with the day-to-day concerns of finance practitioners. Other books in this continuing series are:

Harold Bierman, Jr.
Implementing Capital Budgeting Techniques, Revised Edition

John D. Finnerty, Andrew J. Kalotay,
and Francis X. Farrell, Jr.
The Financial Manager's Guide to Evaluating Bond Refunding Opportunities

Dennis E. Logue
Pension Fund Management

Ronald W. Masulis
The Debt/Equity Choice

Charles W. Smithson, Clifford W. Smith, and
D. Sykes Wilford
Financial Risk Management

The FMA Series is part of the larger Institutional Investor Series in Finance.

The costs of research and development that made the Financial Management Association Survey and Synthesis Series possible were underwritten in part by support provided to the Financial Management Association by United Airlines, the Federal Reserve Bank of Philadelphia, and Ameritech.

INTERNATIONAL CORPORATE FINANCE
Second Edition

Alan C. Shapiro

BALLINGER PUBLISHING COMPANY
Cambridge, Massachusetts
A Subsidiary of Harper & Row, Publishers, Inc.

International Standard Book Number: 0-88730-358-7

Library of Congress Catalog Card Number: 88-24143

Printed in the United States of America

Library of Congress Cataloging-in-Publication Data

Shapiro, Alan C.

International corporate finance/Alan C. Shapiro. — 2nd ed.

p. cm. — (Financial Management Association survey and
  synthesis series) (Institutional investor series in finance)
Bibliography: p.
Includes index.
ISBN 0-88730-358-7
1. International business enterprises — Finance. I. Title.
II. Series. III. Series: Institutional investor series in finance.
HG4027.5.S46 1988   88-24143
658.1′599—dc19   CIP

Contents

Chapter 1	Introduction	1
	Relationship to Domestic Financial Management	2
	The Process of Overseas Expansion	6
Chapter 2	Foreign Exchange Risk Management	13
	Key Equilibrium Relationships	13
	Currency Forecasting	18
	Measuring Foreign Exchange Risk	23
	The Hedging Decision	33
	Managing Exchange Risk	49
Chapter 3	International Working Capital Management	69
	International Cash Management	69
	Accounts Receivable Management	77
	Inventory Management	80
	Short-Term Financing	82
	Managing Intracorporate Fund Flows	87

Chapter 4 Foreign Investment Analysis   99

　　　　　Capital Budgeting for the Multinational
　　　　　Corporation   99

　　　　　Political Risk Measurement and Management   111

　　　　　The Cost of Capital for Foreign Investments   116

　　　　　Corporate Strategy and Foreign Investment   123

Chapter 5 Financing Foreign Operations   131

　　　　　International Financing and International
　　　　　Financial Markets   131

　　　　　The Euromarkets   140

　　　　　Special Financing Vehicles   152

Chapter 6 Designing A Global Financing Strategy   163

　　　　　Minimizing Expected After-Tax Financing Costs 164

　　　　　Reducing Operating Risks   168

　　　　　Establishing a Worldwide Financial Structure   173

Chapter 7 Summary and Conclusions   177

Notes   181

Bibliography   191

Index   197

About the Author   213

1

Introduction

As the multinational corporation (MNC) becomes the norm rather than the exception, a need to internationalize the tools of domestic financial analysis becomes apparent. The aim of this book is to provide a conceptual framework within which to analyze the key financial decisions of the multinational firm.

The ability to move people, money, and material on a global basis enables the multinational corporation to be more than the sum of its parts. By operating in different countries, the MNC can access segmented capital markets to lower its overall cost of capital, shift profits to lower its taxes, and take advantage of international diversification to reduce the riskiness of its earnings. At the same time, the MNC is subject to a variety of factors that purely domestic firms encounter rarely, if ever. These factors include multiple currencies with frequent exchange rate changes and varying rates of inflation, differing tax systems, multiple money markets, exchange controls, segmented capital markets, and political risks such as nationalization or expropriation.

To properly analyze and balance these international risks and rewards, the lessons learned from domestic corporate finance must be used. The key decision elements—risk and return—are the same in both domestic and international contexts, and so can be examined using the same valuation framework. It also helps to understand the process of overseas expansion.

Relationship to Domestic Financial Management

Recent years have seen an abundance of new research in the area of international corporate finance. The major thrust of this body of work has been to apply the methodology and logic of financial economics to the study of key international financial decisions. Financial economics emphasizes the use of economic analysis to understand the basic workings of financial markets, particularly the measurement and pricing of risk and the intertemporal allocation of funds. Critical problem areas such as foreign exchange risk management and foreign investment analysis have benefited from the insights of such a discipline.

By focusing on the behavior of financial markets and their participants rather than on how to solve specific problems, we can derive fundamental principles of valuation and, from them, develop superior courses of action—much as a good engineer applies the basic laws of physics to design better functioning products and processes. We can also better gauge the validity of generally accepted financial practices by seeing whether their underlying assumptions are consistent with our knowledge of financial markets and valuation principles.

Arbitrage, Market Efficiency, and Capital Asset Pricing

Three concepts arising in financial economics have proved especially valuable in developing a theoretical foundation for international corporate finance: arbitrage, market efficiency, and capital asset pricing.

Traditionally, *arbitrage* has been defined as the purchase of securities or commodities on one market for immediate resale on another in order to profit from a price discrepancy. Under this definition, the positions being taken by investors are close to riskless. More recently, arbitrage has been used to describe a broader range of financial activities. Tax arbitrage, for example, involves the shifting of gains or losses from one tax jurisdiction to another or from one category of income to another in order to profit from differences in tax rates. Even more important from the standpoint in this text is the extension of arbitrage to include trading activities that involve risk. Risk arbitrage, sometimes termed speculation, has been used to describe the process which ensures that in equilibrium, risk-adjusted returns on different assets are equal, unless market imperfections hinder this adjustment process. In fact, it is the process of risk arbitrage, fueled by new information or differences of opinion, that ensures market efficiency.

An *efficient financial market* is one in which new information is incorporated rapidly in the prices of traded securities. Thus, price changes at any moment must be due solely to the arrival of new information. As new information that is useful for profitable trading activities arrives at random (if not random, the information would be neither new nor useful), price changes must follow a random walk. In other words, in an efficient market, price changes from one period to the next are independent of past price changes and are no more predictable than is new information. Consistent with this implication, numerous studies of U.S. and overseas financial markets have shown that prices of traded securities follow random walks.

Market efficiency is a powerful concept. Yet it is impossible to prove or disprove the efficient market hypothesis. There is always the possibility that someone, somewhere, can develop a model or find a relationship that leads to superior forecasting ability. All that can be done is to test alternative forecasting models and determine whether the results support (but not prove) the efficient market hypothesis. So far at least, the results of tests that have been performed appear to be consistent with market efficiency.

Capital asset pricing refers to how securities are valued given their anticipated risks. Generally, it is agreed that investors require higher returns on riskier investments. Financial economists have probably devoted more effort to measuring risk and establishing the tradeoff between risk and expected return (that is, the price of risk) than to any other topic. The outcome of this research has been to posit specific relationships among diversification, risk, and required return that are formalized now in the *capital asset pricing model* (CAPM) and the more general *arbitrage pricing theory* (APT).[1] Risk itself is assumed to depend on the variability of returns; the more highly variable the return, the riskier the security.

The CAPM and the APT are based on the idea that the total variability of an asset's returns can be attributed to two sources: (1) marketwide influences, such as the level of interest rates or growth in Gross National Product, that affect all assets to some extent; and (2) other risks, such as a strike or a new patentable invention, that are specific to a given firm. The former type of risk is usually termed *systematic* or *market* risk, and the latter *unsystematic* or *diversifiable* risk. It can be shown that unsystematic risk is largely irrelevant to the investor who holds a highly diversified portfolio because, on average, the effects of such disturbances can be expected to cancel out in the portfolio. On the other hand, no matter how well diversified the investment portfolio, systematic risk, by definition, cannot be eliminated, and thus the investor must be compensated for bearing this risk. The distinction between systematic and unsystematic risks provides the theoretical foundation for the pricing of risk in the multinational corporation.

The Importance of Total Risk

Although the message of both the CAPM and the APT is that only the systematic component of risk will be rewarded with a risk premium, this does not mean that total risk is unimportant to the value of the firm. While systematic risk affects the appropriate discount rate, total risk may have a negative impact on the firm's *expected* cash flows.

The inverse relation between risk and expected cash flows arises because financial distress, which is more likely to occur for firms with high *total* risk, can impose costs on customers, suppliers, and employees, thereby affecting their willingness to commit themselves to relationships with the firm.[2] The result is lower sales and higher costs. Consequently, any action taken by a firm that decreases its total risk will improve its sales and cost outlook, thereby increasing its expected cash flows.

The adverse effects of total risk on sales and costs provide justification for the range of corporate hedging activities in which multinational firms engage that are designed to reduce total risk. This book focuses on those risks that appear to be more international in nature such as inflation risk, exchange risk, and political risk. Appearances, however, can be deceiving, for these risks also affect firms that do business in only one country. Moreover, as mentioned earlier, international diversification actually may allow firms to reduce the total risk they face, giving rise to another source of value and a further rationale for foreign expansion.

The Global Financial Marketplace

Market efficiency has been greatly facilitated by the marriage of computers and telecommunications, which has constructed an electronic infrastructure that melds the world into one global market for ideas, data, and capital, all moving at almost the speed of light to any part of the planet. Today there are more than 200,000 computer screens in hundreds of trading rooms, in dozens of nations, which light up to display an unending flow of news. It takes about two minutes between the time the president, a prime minister, or a central banker makes a statement and the time traders buy or sell currency, stocks, or bonds based on their evaluation of the effect of that policy on the market.

The result is a continuing global referendum on a nation's economic policies, which is the final determinant of the value of its currency. Just as we learn from television the winner of a U.S. presidential election weeks before the Electoral College even assembles, so also we learn instantly from the foreign exchange market what the world thinks of our announced economic policies even before they are implemented. In a way, the financial market is a form of economic free speech. Although many politicians do not like what it is saying, the market's judgments are clear eyed and hard nosed. The market knows that there are no miracle drugs that can replace sound fiscal and monetary policies. Thus, cosmetic political fixes will exacerbate, not alleviate, a falling currency.

The Role of the Financial Executive in an Efficient Market

Despite widespread evidence of market efficiency and investor rationality, many companies persist in expending real resources in attempts to fool shareholders or to provide them with something, such as corporate diversification, which is probably unnecessary. For instance, a large number of U.S. firms agonized over the decision of whether to switch to the LIFO (last-in, first-out) method of inventory valuation during the period of rapid inflation in the 1970s. Switching to LIFO when prices are rising produces a reduction in reported earnings but an increase in cash flow due to tax write-offs. If investors focus on cash flows rather than on accounting income, then the basic rule to follow whenever there is a conflict between the two is to "take the money and run." The irrelevance of this agonizing was underscored by presentations in publications such as *Business Week* of LIFO-adjusted earnings of those firms clinging to the FIFO (first-in, first-out) method of inventory valuation. The fundamental insight into financial management to be gained from this and similar evidence is the following: Attempts to increase the value of a firm by purely financial measures or accounting manipulations are unlikely to succeed unless there are capital market imperfections or asymmetries in tax regulations.

Rather than downgrading the role of the financial executive, the net result of these research findings has been to focus attention on those areas and circumstances in which financial decisions can have a measurable impact. The key areas appear to be evaluation and control of operations, capital budgeting, working capital management, and tax management. The circumstances for the financial executive to be aware of include capital market imperfections (primarily caused by government regulations), and asymmetries in the tax treatment of different types and sources of revenues and costs.

The value of good financial management is enhanced in the international arena because of the much greater likelihood of encountering market imperfections and multiple tax rates. Moreover, the greater complexity of international operations is likely to increase the payoffs from a knowledgeable and sophisticated approach to internationalizing the traditional areas of financial management.

The Process of Overseas Expansion

Studies of corporate expansion overseas indicate that firms become multinational by degree, with foreign direct investment being only a late step in a process that begins with exports. For most companies, the *internationalization* process does not occur through conscious design, at least in the early stages, but rather is the unplanned result of a series of corporate responses to a variety of threats and opportunities that appear at random abroad. From a broader perspective, however, the *multinationalization* of firms can be seen as the inevitable outcome of the competitive strivings of members of oligopolistic industries, with each member trying to both create and exploit monopolistic product and factor advantages internationally while simultaneously attempting to reduce the perceived competitive threats posed by the other members of its industry.

To meet these challenges, companies gradually increase their commitment to international business, developing strategies that are progressively more elaborate and sophisticated. The sequence normally involves exporting, setting up a foreign sales subsidiary, possible licensing agreements and, eventually, foreign production. This evolutionary approach to expanding overseas can be viewed as a risk-minimizing response to operating in a highly uncertain foreign environment. By internationalizing in phases, a firm can gradually move from a relatively "low risk–low return," export-oriented strategy to a "higher risk–higher return" strategy emphasizing international production. In effect, the firm is investing in information, learning enough at each stage to significantly improve its chances for success at the succeeding stage. The usual sequence of overseas expansion is depicted in Figure 1-1.

Exporting

Firms facing highly uncertain demand abroad will typically begin by exporting to a foreign market. The advantages of exporting are significant: capital requirements and start-up costs are minimal, risk is low, and profits are immediate. Potential learning is great with regard to present and future supply-and-demand conditions,

Figure 1-1. Typical Foreign Expansion Sequence

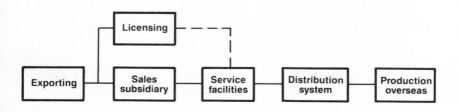

Source: Alan C. Shapiro, *Multinational Financial Management*, (Boston: Allyn and Bacon, 2nd edition 1986), p. 6.

competition, channels of distribution, payment conventions, and financial institutions and techniques. Building on prior successes, companies then expand their marketing organizations abroad, switching from using export agents and other intermediaries to dealing directly with foreign agents and distributors. As uncertainty is reduced through increased communication with customers, the firm might establish its own sales subsidiary and new service facilities, such as a warehouse, with the culmination of these marketing activities being the control of its own distribution system.

Overseas Production

There is a major drawback to exporting: an inability to realize the full sales potential of a product. By manufacturing abroad, a company can more easily keep abreast of market developments, adapting its products and production schedules to changing local tastes and conditions while, simultaneously, providing more comprehensive after-sales service.

Moreover, establishing local production facilities demonstrates a greater commitment to the local market and an increased assurance of supply stability. This is particularly important for firms that produce intermediate goods for sale to other companies. A case in point is SKF, the Swedish ball bearing manufacturer, which was forced to manufacture in the United States to guarantee that its product, a crucial component in military equipment, would be available when needed. The U.S. Pentagon would not permit its suppliers of military hardware to be dependent on imported ball bearings, shipment of which could be halted in wartime and in any case, are always subject to the vagaries of ocean shipping. Concern over the delays caused by ocean transportation also played a role in Volkswagen's decision to begin automobile production in the United States. Ninety days elapsed from the time when a change in U.S. demand was first apparent until the time when VW Rabbits could be landed in the United States; this time period included shifting production schedules at Wolfsburg, the West German plant, packing and shipping the cars across the Atlantic, unloading them, and going through customs.

Thus, most firms selling in foreign markets eventually find themselves forced to manufacture abroad. Foreign production covers a wide spectrum of activities, from repairing, packaging, and finishing to processing, assembly, and full manufacture. Firms typically begin with the simpler stages and progressively integrate their manufacturing activities backwards.

Since the optimal foreign market entry strategy can change over time, firms must must continually monitor and evaluate the factors that bear on the effectiveness of their current entry strategy. New information and market perceptions change the risk-return trade-off for a given entry strategy, leading to a sequence of preferred entry modes, each one adapted on the basis of prior experience, to sustain and strengthen the firm's market position over time.

Associated with a firm's decision to produce abroad is the question of whether to *create* its own affiliates or *acquire* going concerns. A major advantage of an acquisition is the capacity to effect a speedy transfer overseas of highly developed but underutilized parent skills, such as a novel production technology. Often, the local firm also provides a ready-made marketing network. This is especially important if the parent is a late entrant to the market. Many firms have also used the acquisition approach to gain knowledge about the local market or a particular technology. The disadvantage, of course, is the cost of acquiring an ongoing company. In general, the larger and more experienced a firm becomes the less frequently it uses acquisitions to expand overseas. Smaller and relatively less experienced firms often turn to acquisitions.

Regardless of its preferences, a firm interested in expanding overseas may have to take the *de novo* road. Michelin, the French radial tiremaker, set up its own facilities in the United States because its tires are built on specially designed equipment; taking over an existing operation would have been out of the question. Similarly, companies moving into developing countries often find they are forced to begin from the ground up, because they are engaged in a line of business that has no local counterpart.

Licensing

An alternative, and at times a precursor, to setting up production facilities abroad is to license a local firm to manufacture the company's products in return for royalties and other forms of payment. The principal advantage of licensing is the minimal investment required. But the corresponding cash flow is also relatively low, and there may be problems in maintaining product quality standards. It may also prove difficult for the multinational firm to garner all the rents associated with its information monopoly if it licenses others to manufacture its products. For one thing, it may be difficult to control exports by the foreign licensee, particularly where (as in Japan) the host government is likely to refuse to sanction any restrictive clauses on sales to foreign markets. Thus, a licensing agreement may lead to the establishment of a competitor in third country markets, with a consequent loss of future revenues to the licensing firm. In addition, the foreign licensee may become such a strong competitor that the licensing firm will have difficulty entering the market when the agreement expires, leading to a further loss of potential profits.

For some firms, licensing alone is the preferred method of penetrating foreign markets. Other firms with diversified, innovative product lines follow a strategy of trading technology for equity plus royalty payments in foreign joint ventures.

A Behavioral Definition of the Multinational Corporation

Regardless of the foreign entry or global expansion strategy pursued, the true multinational corporation can be characterized more by its state of mind than by the size and worldwide dispersion of its assets. Rather than confine its search to domestic plant sites, the multinational firm asks "Where in the world should we build that plant?" Similarly, multinational marketing management seeks global, not domestic, market segments to penetrate, while multinational financial management does not limit its search for capital or investment opportunities to any single, national, financial market. Hence, the essential element that distinguishes the true multinational is its commitment to seeking out and undertaking investment, marketing, and financing opportunities on a global, not domestic, basis. Moreover, in this world-oriented corporation, a person's passport is not the criterion for promotion. Nor is a firm's citizenship a critical determinant of its success. Success depends on a new breed of businessperson: the global manager.

The Global Manager

In a world in which change is the rule and not the exception, the key to international competitiveness is the ability of management to adjust to change and volatility at an ever faster rate. The risks are higher in such a world, but so is the capacity to manage the risks—using strategic tools ranging from global manufacturing networks to product innovation to currency swaps—and to profit from them.

This means the new global manager needs detailed knowledge of his or her own operation. The manager must know how to make the product, where the raw materials and parts come from, how they get there, the alternatives, where the funds come from, and what their changing relative value does to the bottom line. The global manager must also understand the political and economic choices facing key nations and how these choices will affect the outcomes of the manager's decisions.

In making decisions for the global company the global manager searches the array of plants in various nations for the most cost-effective mix of supplies, components, transport, and funds. And the constant awareness is that the choices change and have to be made again and again.

The problem of constant change disturbs some managers. It always has. But today's global manager has to anticipate it, understand it, deal with it, and turn it to his or her company's advantage. The payoff to thinking globally is a quality of decision-making that enhances the firm's prospects for survival, growth, and profitability in the evolving world economy.

2

Foreign Exchange Risk Management

Foreign exchange risk management is one traditional area of concern that is receiving even more attention today. Several key equilibrium relationships—between interest rates, spot and forward exchange rates, and inflation rates—form the basis for much of the analysis in this book.

Key Equilibrium Relationships

In competitive markets—those characterized by numerous buyers and sellers having low-cost access to information—exchange-adjusted prices of identical tradable goods and financial assets must be within transactions costs of equality worldwide. This idea is referred to as the *law of one price*. This law is enforced by international arbitrageurs who, by following the dictum of "buy low, sell high," prevent all but trivial deviations from equality. Similarly, in the absence of market imperfections, risk-adjusted expected returns on financial assets in different markets should be equal.

Five key theoretical economic relationships, depicted in Figure 2–1, result from these arbitrage activities:

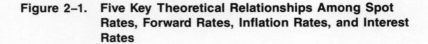

Figure 2–1. Five Key Theoretical Relationships Among Spot Rates, Forward Rates, Inflation Rates, and Interest Rates

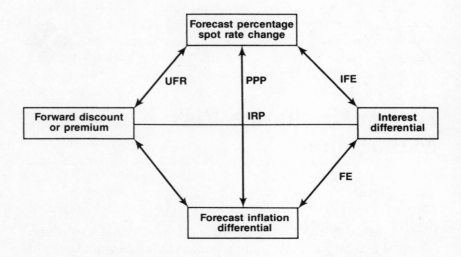

1. Purchasing power parity (PPP).
2. Fisher effect (FE).
3. International Fisher effect (IFE).
4. Interest rate parity (IRP).
5. Forward rates as unbiased predictors of future spot rates (UFR).

This set of arbitrage relationships emphasizes the links among prices, spot exchange rates, interest rates, and forward rates. The common denominator is the adjustment of the various rates and prices to inflation. According to modern monetary theory, inflation is the logical outcome of an expansion of the money supply in excess of real output growth. Although this view of the origin of inflation is not accepted universally, it has a solid microeconomic foundation. In particular, it is a basic precept of price theory that, as the supply of one commodity increases relative to supplies of all other commodities, the price of the first commodity must decline relative to the prices of other commodities. For example, a bumper crop of corn should cause corn's value in exchange—its exchange rate—to decline. Similarly, as the supply of money increases relative to the supply of goods and services, the purchasing power of money—the exchange rate between money and goods—must decline.

The mechanism underlying this relationship is simple and direct. Suppose, for example, that the supply of dollars exceeds the amount that individuals desire to hold. In order to reduce their excess holdings of money, individuals increase their spending on goods, services, and securities, causing domestic prices to rise.

A further link in the causal chain that relates money supply growth, inflation, interest rates, and exchange rates is the notion that money is neutral—that is, money should have no impact on real variables. Thus, for example, a 10 percent increase in the supply of money relative to the demand for money should cause prices to rise by 10 percent. The neutrality of money has important implications for international finance. Specifically, although a change in the quantity of money will affect prices and exchange rates, it should not affect the rate at which domestic goods are exchanged for foreign goods or the rate at which goods today are exchanged for goods in the future. The neutrality of money in international exchange and in intertemporal exchange are formalized as *purchasing power parity* (PPP) and the *Fisher* and *international Fisher effects* (FE and IFE), respectively.

The international analogue to inflation is home currency depreciation relative to foreign currencies. Inflation involves a change in the exchange rate between the home currency and domestic goods, whereas home currency depreciation—a decline in the foreign currency value of the home currency—results in a change in the exchange rate between the home currency and foreign goods.

That inflation and currency depreciation are related is no accident. Excess money supply growth, through its impact on the rate of aggregate spending, affects the demand for goods produced abroad as well. This, in turn, changes the domestic demand for foreign currencies and, consequently, the foreign exchange value of the domestic currency. Thus, the rate of domestic inflation and changes in the exchange rate are determined jointly by the rate of domestic money growth relative to the growth of the amount that people, in domestic and foreign countries, want to hold.

If international arbitrage enforces the law of one price, then the exchange rate between the home currency and domestic goods must equal the exchange rate between the home currency and foreign goods. Thus, if one dollar buys a pound of bread in the United States, it also should buy one pound of bread in Great Britain. For this to happen, the foreign exchange rate must change by (approximately) the difference between the domestic and foreign rates of inflation. This is *purchasing power parity*.[1]

Similarly, the *nominal* interest rate, the price quoted on lending and borrowing transactions, determines the exchange rate between current and future dollars (or any other currency). For example, an interest rate of 10 percent on a one-year loan means that 1 dollar today is being exchanged for 1.1 dollars a year from now. But what really matters according to the *Fisher* and *international Fisher effects* is the exchange rate between current and future purchasing power, as measured by the *real* interest rate. Simply put, the lender is concerned with how many more goods can be obtained in the future by forgoing consumption today, while the borrower wants to know how much future consumption must be sacrificed to obtain more goods today. The concern with the real interest rate holds regardless of whether the borrower and lender are located in the same or different countries. As a result, if the exchange rate between current and future goods—the real interest rate—varies from one country to the next, arbitrage between domestic and foreign capital markets, in the form of international capital flows, should occur. These flows will tend to equalize real interest rates across countries.[2] For example, if real interest rates in West Germany and the United States are 3 percent and 4 percent, respectively, money will flow from West Germany to the United States to take advantage of the higher real return in the United States. The resulting shift of capital, which raises the real return in West Germany and lowers it in the United States, will continue until the real interest rate is the same in both countries, ending up somewhere between 3 percent and 4 percent.

Interest rate parity (IRP) says that the forward exchange rate on the currency bearing a lower interest rate should be at a premium relative to its spot value, where the exchange rates are stated in terms of the currency of the higher interest rate country. More specifically, in an efficient market with no transaction costs, the interest differential should equal the forward differential (the difference between the forward and spot rates divided by the spot rate). Otherwise a riskless arbitrage opportunity would exist. Similarly, if most of the variability in exchange rates is unsystematic (as seems to be the case), arbitrage should ensure that the forward differential is approximately equal to the expected change in the exchange rate. In other words, *forward rates should be unbiased predictors of future spot rates.*[3]

The technical description of these five equilibrium relationships is summarized in Figure 2-2.

Figure 2-2. Key Parity Relations in International Finance

1. Purchasing power parity

$$\frac{e_t}{e_0} = \frac{1 + i_{h,t}}{1 + i_{f,t}}$$

where
- e_t = the home currency value of the foreign currency at time t.
- e_0 = the home currency value of the foreign currency at time 0.
- $i_{h,t}$ = the amount of domestic inflation between times 0 and t.
- $i_{f,t}$ = the amount of foreign inflation between times 0 and t.

2. Fisher effect

$$1 + r = (1 + a)(1 + i)$$

where
- r = the nominal rate of interest.
- a = the real rate of interest.
- i = the rate of expected inflation.

3. International Fisher effect

$$\frac{1 + r_{h,t}}{1 + r_{f,t}} = \frac{e_t}{e_0}$$

where $r_{h,\ t}$ = the t-period home currency interest rate.
$r_{f,t}$ = the t-period foreign currency interest rate.

4. Interest rate parity

$$\frac{1 + r_{h,t}}{1 + r_{f,t}} = \frac{f_t}{e_0}$$

where f_t = the forward rate for delivery of one unit of foreign currency at time t.

5. The forward rate as an unbiased predictor of the future spot rate

$$f_t = e_t$$

where e_t = the expected home currency value of the foreign currency at time t.

Currency Forecasting

Forecasting exchange rates has become an occupational hazard for financial executives of multinational corporations. The potential for periodic—and unpredictable—government intervention makes currency forecasting all the more difficult. But this has not dampened the enthusiasm for currency forecasts nor the willingness of economists and others to supply them. Unfortunately, though, enthusiasm and willingness are not sufficient conditions for success.

Requirements for Successful Currency Forecasting

Currency forecasting can lead to consistent profits only if the forecaster meets at least one of the following four criteria:[4] He or she (1) has exclusive use of a superior forecasting model; (2) has consistent access to information before other investors; (3) exploits small, temporary deviations from equilibrium; or (4) can predict the nature of government intervention in the foreign exchange market.

The first two conditions are self-correcting. Successful forecasting breeds imitators, while the second situation is unlikely to last long in the highly informed world of international finance. The third situation describes how foreign exchange traders actually earn their living, and also why deviations from equilibrium are not likely to last long. The fourth situation is the one worth searching out. Countries that insist on fixing, or at least managing, their exchange rates, and are willing to take losses to achieve their target rates, present speculators with potentially profitable opportunities. Simply put, consistently profitable predictions are possible in the long run only if it is not necessary to outguess the market to win.

As a general rule, when forecasting in a fixed-rate system, the focus must be on the governmental decision-making structure because the decision to devalue or revalue at a given time is clearly political. During the Bretton Woods system, many speculators did quite well by "stepping into the shoes of the key decisionmakers" to forecast their likely behavior.

In the case of a floating rate system, where government intervention is sporadic or nonexistent, currency prognosticators have the choice of using either market- or model-based forecasts, neither of which guarantees success.

Market-Based Forecasts

So far, we have identified several equilibrium relationships that should exist between exchange rates and interest rates. The empirical evidence on these relationships implies that, in general, the financial markets of developed countries efficiently incorporate expected currency changes in the cost of money and forward exchange. This means that currency forecasts can be obtained by extracting the predictions already embodied in interest and forward rates.

Forward Rates

Market-based forecasts of exchange rate changes can be derived most simply from current forward rates. Specifically, f_1—the forward rate for one period from now—will usually suffice for an unbiased estimate of the spot rate as of that date. In other words, f_1 should equal e_1, where e_1 is the expected future spot rate.

Interest Rates

Although forward rates provide simple and easy to use currency forecasts, their forecasting horizon is limited to about one year because of the general absence of longer-term forward contracts. Interest rate differentials can be used to supply exchange rate predictions beyond one year. For example, suppose five-year interest rates on dollars and deutsche marks are 12 percent and 8 percent, respectively. If the current spot rate for the deutsche mark (DM) is \$0.60 and the (unknown) value of the DM in five years is e_5, then \$1.00 invested today in deutsche marks will be worth $(1.08)^5 e_5/0.6$ dollars at the end of five years; if invested in the dollar security it will be worth $(1.12)^5$ in five years. The market's forecast of e_5 can be found by assuming that investors demand equal returns on dollar and DM securities, or

$$(1.08)^5 e_5/0.6 = (1.12)^5.$$

Thus, the five-year DM spot rate implied by the relative interest rates is $e_5 = \$0.7196$ $(0.60 \times 1.12^5/1.08^5)$.

Model-Based Forecasts

The two principal model-based approaches to currency prediction are known as fundamental analysis and technical analysis. Each approach has its advocates and detractors.

Fundamental Analysis

Fundamental analysis is the most common approach to forecasting future exchange rates. It relies on painstaking examination of the macroeconomic variables and policies that are likely to influence a currency's prospects. The variables examined include relative inflation and interest rates, national income growth rates, and changes in money supplies. The interpretation of these variables and their implications for future exchange rates depend on the analyst's model of exchange rate determination.

Most analysts treat currency values as determined by demand and supply flows in the foreign exchange market. In this *traditional flow model* of currency determination, the analysis of the different macroeconomic variables usually centers on their balance-of-payments impact. The balance of payments consists of the current account, which incorporates the trade balance, and the capital account. The forecaster attempts to anticipate the direction and magnitude of imbalances that may occur in each account and in the overall balance. By successfully estimating the overall balance, the demand and supply for a currency can be determined, as well as—it is hoped—its future value. This latter step involves estimating the exchange rate at which supply just equals demand—when any current account imbalance is just matched by a net capital flow.

The view that exchange rates are set in flow markets is rejected by the *asset market model*. According to this model, an exchange rate is simply the relative price of two assets—one country's currency in terms of another's—which is determined in the same manner as are the prices of other assets such as stocks, bonds, gold, or real estate. Asset prices, unlike the prices of services or products with short storage lives, are influenced comparatively little by current events. They are determined rather by the existing quantities of the assets and by people's willingness to hold them. For example, while frost in Florida can bump up the price of oranges, it should have little impact on the price of the citrus groves producing the oranges; instead, the values of these groves are governed by longer-term expectations about the supply and demand for oranges.

Similarly, because the outstanding stock of financial assets denominated in a given currency, say, the dollar, is unlikely to change radically over short periods, the dollar's value today depends on whether or not—and how strongly—people still want the amount of dollar-denominated assets they held yesterday. The desire to hold a currency, in turn, depends critically on expectations of factors—such as monetary policy and economic growth—that can affect the relative supply and demand for the currency in the future; that is, what matters is not just what is happening today but what markets expect will happen in the future. Thus, currency values are set by expectations of their countries' future economic prospects rather than by contemporaneous flows of exports and imports. Contrary to the traditional flow approach, the asset market model predicts that there should be no determinate relationship between exchange rates and movements in either the trade or the current account balance. This is indeed the case, as shown in Figure 2–3. For example, from 1976 until 1980, the value of the dollar declined as the current account deficit for the United States first worsened and then improved, while from 1980 to 1985, the dollar strengthened even as the current account steadily deteriorated.

As currencies are assets, the modern theory of asset price determination in efficient markets has an important implication for those interested in assessing currency values: Exchange rates will fluctuate randomly as market participants assess and then react to new information, much as security and commodity prices in other asset markets respond to news. Thus, exchange rate movements are unpredictable; otherwise, it would be possible to earn arbitrage profits. Such profits could not persist in a market such as the foreign exchange market, which is characterized by free entry and exit and by an almost unlimited amount of resources that participants are willing to commit in pursuit of profit opportunities.

Technical Analysis

Technical analysis is the antithesis of fundamental analysis in that it focuses exclusively on past price and volume movements—while totally ignoring economic and political factors—to forecast currency winners and losers. Success depends on whether

Figure 2–3. The Balance of Payments and the Exchange Rate

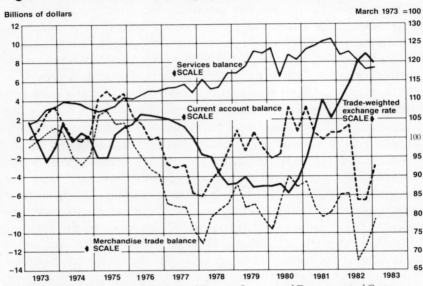

Billions of dollars   March 1973 = 100

Source: Board of Governors of the Federal Reserve System and Department of Commerce, Bureau of Economic Analysis, *Survey of Current Business* (1983).

technical analysts can discover price patterns that repeat themselves and therefore are useful for forecasting.

There are two primary methods of technical analysis: charting and trend analysis. Chartists examine bar charts or use more sophisticated computer-based extrapolation techniques to find recurring price patterns. They then issue buy or sell recommendations if prices diverge from their past pattern. Trend-following systems seek to identify price trends via various mathematical computations.

Model Evaluation

The possibility that either fundamental or technical analysis can be used to profitably forecast exchange rates is inconsistent with the efficient market hypothesis, which says that current exchange rates should reflect all publicly available information.

Despite the theoretical skepticism over successful currency forecasting, a study of fourteen forecast advisory services by

Richard Levich indicates that the profits associated with using several of these forecasts seem too good to be explained by chance.[5] Of course, if the forward rate contains a risk premium, these returns would have to be adjusted for the risks borne by speculators. It is also questionable whether currency forecasters would continue selling their information rather than acting on it themselves if they truly believed it could yield excess *risk-adjusted* returns.

Measuring Foreign Exchange Risk

As a result of its investment, production, and other operating decisions, a firm generates both a current structure of assets and liabilities, and a stream of expected future cash flows.[6] The most critical aspect of foreign exchange risk management is to incorporate currency change expectations into *all* basic corporate decisions affecting cash flow and financial structure. Once that is done, management is then in a position to decide whether to "self-insure" the risks of unanticipated (and largely diversifiable) currency fluctuations or to "lay them off" in financial markets.

In making this decision, the firm must know what is at risk. However, there is a major discrepancy between accounting practice and economic reality in terms of measuring exposure, which is the degree to which a company is affected by exchange rate changes.

Foreign exchange risk management has been dominated by accountants and others who rely on a "balance sheet" approach to measure exposure to exchange rate changes. Those who use an accounting definition—whether FASB-8, FASB-52, or some other method—divide the balance sheet's foreign currency-denominated assets and liabilities into those accounts that will be affected by exchange rate changes and those that will not.[7] In contrast, economic theory focuses on the impact of an exchange rate change on future cash flows; that is, *economic exposure* is based on the extent to which the value of the firm—as measured by the present value of its expected future cash flows—will change when exchange rates change. *Exchange risk*, in turn, is defined as the variability in the value of the firm that is caused by uncertain exchange rate changes. Thus, exchange risk is viewed as the possibility that currency fluctuations can alter the expected amounts of the firm's future cash flows.

Economic Versus Accounting Values

This book uses an economic definition of exchange risk based on market value, assuming that management's goal is to maximize the value of the firm. Whether management actually behaves in this fashion has been debated vigorously. Clearly, some managers will prefer to pursue other objectives. In fact, many financial managers probably consider reducing the variability of translated earnings to be the principal function of exchange risk management, as evidenced by the earlier widespread practice of hedging FASB-8 earnings. Nevertheless, the assumption that management attempts to maximize risk-adjusted after-tax cash flow remains standard in much of the finance literature. Moreover, the principle of shareholder wealth maximization provides a rational guide to financial decisionmaking.

The companion to value maximization is market efficiency. If the capital market did not rationally price the firm's securities, managers would be hard pressed to design a value-maximizing foreign exchange strategy. Fortunately, there is strong evidence that capital markets are relatively sophisticated in responding to publicly available information. Most of the large body of research on financial markets suggests that, when accounting numbers diverge significantly from cash flows, changes in security prices generally reflect changes in cash flows rather than reported earnings.

The basic problem with the accounting approach to measuring exposure is that book values and market values typically differ, so that the change in net worth produced by a movement in exchange rates often bears little relationship to the change in the value of the firm. But no matter how careful we are in measuring the true economic consequences of currency changes for a given firm, we still will have a fundamentally flawed picture of the firm's actual exposure if we ignore the implications of two key equilibrium relationships observed in international financial markets: purchasing power parity and the international Fisher effect.

As seen earlier, exchange rate changes do not just happen; according to the theory of purchasing power parity, changes in the ratio of domestic to foreign prices will cause offsetting changes in the exchange rate so as to maintain the relative purchasing powers of the currencies involved. Although purchasing power parity does not hold exactly, a large portion of exchange rate changes are explained by equal and opposite changes in national price levels. Moreover, the international Fisher effect says that returns on assets being held and the costs of liabilities incurred (should) implicitly incorporate anticipated currency changes.

Only by explicitly recognizing the implications of these equilibrium relationships, and deviations from them, for the estimation and valuation of future cash flows can we hope to come to grips with the problem of determining a firm's true economic exposure.

Economic Consequences of Exchange Rate Changes

Economic exposure to exchange risk, which was defined earlier as the extent to which the firm's value will be affected by changes in exchange rates, can be separated into two components: transaction exposure and real operating exposure. *Transaction exposure* is the possibility of incurring future exchange gains or losses on transactions already entered into and denominated in a foreign currency. Some of these transactions, including foreign currency-denominated debt and accounts receivable, are listed on the firm's balance sheet. But other obligations, such as contracts for future sales or purchases, are not. Although transaction exposure is often included under accounting exposure, it is more properly a cash flow exposure and hence part of economic exposure.

Real operating exposure arises because currency fluctuations, together with price changes, can alter the amounts and riskiness of a company's future revenue and cost streams (that is, its operating cash flows). Consequently, measuring a firm's operating exposure requires detailed knowledge of its operations and their exchange rate sensitivity. Such a measurement also requires a longer-term perspective, viewing the firm as an ongoing concern with operations whose cost and price competitiveness could be affected by exchange rate changes.

The measurement of economic exposure is made especially difficult because it is impossible to assess the effects of an exchange rate change without simultaneously considering the impact on cash flows of the underlying relative rates of inflation associated with each currency. The concept of the *real* exchange rate may help clarify the discussion of exposure. The real exchange rate is defined as the *nominal*, or actual, exchange rate adjusted for changes in the relative purchasing power of each currency since some base period. Specifically, the real exchange rate in period t, e'_t, is defined as

$$e'_t = \frac{e_t(1 + i_f)}{(1 + i_h)}$$

where e_t is the period t home currency price of one unit of the foreign currency, i_f is the amount of foreign inflation from 0 to t, and i_h is the amount of domestic inflation from 0 to t. If changes in the nominal rate are fully offset by changes in the relative price levels between the two countries, then the real exchange rate remains unchanged. Alternatively, a change in the real exchange rate is equivalent to a deviation from PPP.

The distinction between the nominal exchange rate and the real exchange rate is important because of their vastly different implications for exchange risk. As we shall see, a dramatic change in the nominal exchange rate accompanied by an equal change in the price level will not alter real cash flows. On the other hand, if the real exchange rate changes, it will cause *relative* price changes—that is, changes in the ratio of prices of individual goods to the general level of prices. For example, in 1974 the price of gas fuels rose by 33.6 percent while the wholesale price index increased by only 8.0 percent. Thus, the year was characterized both by general inflation and by an increase in the relative price of oil. As might be expected, the press frequently confused the two events and attributed the effects of an increase in the relative price of oil to inflation. It is these relative price changes, not price level changes per se, that cause exchange risk.

Inflation and Exchange Risk

Let us begin by holding relative prices constant and looking only at the effects of general inflation. This means that if the inflation rate is 10 percent, the price of every good in the economy rises by 10 percent. In addition, we initially assume that all goods are traded in a competitive world market without transaction costs, tariffs, or taxes of any kind. Given these conditions, economic theory tells us that the law of one price must prevail; that is, the price of any good, measured in a common currency, must be equal in all countries.

If the law of one price holds, and if there is no variation in the relative prices of goods or services, then the rate of change in the exchange rate must equal the difference between the inflation rates in the two countries. But purchasing power parity does not imply that exchange rate changes will necessarily be small or easy to forecast. If a country has high and unpredictable inflation, as in the case of Brazil, its exchange rate also will fluctuate randomly.

Nonetheless, without relative price changes, a multinational company faces no real operating exchange risk. As long as the firm avoids contracts that are fixed in foreign currency terms, its foreign cash flows will vary with the foreign rate of inflation. Because the exchange rate also depends on the difference between foreign and domestic rates of inflation, the movement of the exchange rate exactly cancels the change in the foreign price level, leaving dollar cash flows unaffected.

Illustration

Apex Spain, the Spanish subsidiary of Apex Company, produces and sells medical imaging devices in Spain. At the current peseta exchange rate of Ptas.1 = $0.01, the devices cost Ptas.40,000 ($400) to produce and they sell for Ptas.100,000 ($1,000). The profit margin of Ptas.60,000 provides a dollar margin of $600. Suppose that Spanish inflation during the year is 20 percent, while the U.S. inflation rate is zero. All prices and costs are assumed to move in line with inflation. Assuming that purchasing power parity holds, the peseta will devalue to $0.0083 (0.01 × 1/1.2). Since the real value of the peseta stays at $0.01 (0.0083 × 1.2/1.0), Apex Spain's dollar profit margin will remain at $600. This is shown in Table 2-1.

Of course, the above conclusion does not hold if the firm enters into contracts fixed in terms of the foreign currency. Examples of such contracts are fixed-rate debt, long-term leases, labor contracts, and rent. However, if the real exchange rate remains constant, the risk introduced by entering into fixed contracts is not exchange risk; it is inflation risk. For instance, an Argentine firm with fixed-rate debt in australs faces the same risk as the

---

Table 2–1. The Effects of Nominal Exchange Rate Changes and Inflation on Apex Spain

Price Level	Spain	U.S.
Beginning of year	100	100
End of year	120	100

	Beginning of year	End of year
Nominal Exchange Rate:	Ptas.1 = $0.01	Ptas.1 = $0.0083
Real Exchange Rate:	Ptas.1 = $0.01	Ptas.1 = $0.0083 × 1.2/1 = $0.01

Profit Impact	Beginning of year Ptas.	U.S.$	End of year Ptas.	U.S.$
Price[a]	100,000	1,000	120,000	1,000
Cost of production	40,000	400	48,000	400
Profit margin	60,000	600	72,000	600

[a]Peseta prices and costs are assumed to increase at the 20 percent rate of Spanish inflation.

---

subsidiary of an American firm with austral debt. If the rate of inflation declines, the real interest cost of the debt rises and the real cash flow of both companies falls. The solution to the problem of inflation risk is to avoid writing contracts fixed in nominal terms in countries with unpredictable inflation. If the contracts are indexed, and if the real exchange rate remains constant, exchange risk is eliminated.

Relative Price Changes and Exchange Risk

In order for there to be real operating exposure, exchange rate changes must *cause* relative price changes within and among countries. Examples of such causation abound. During the late 1970s, for example, worldwide demand for Swiss franc-denominated assets caused the Swiss franc to appreciate in real terms. As a result, Swiss watchmakers were squeezed. Because of competition from Japanese companies, Swiss firms could not significantly raise the dollar price of watches sold in the United States. Yet, at the same time, the *dollar* cost of Swiss labor was rising because the franc wage rate was unchanged, while the franc was appreciating against the dollar.

American companies faced similar problems when the real value of the dollar began rising against other currencies during the early 1980s. U.S. exporters found themselves with the Hobson's choice of keeping dollar prices constant and losing sales volume (because foreign currency prices rose in line with the appreciating dollar) or setting prices in the foreign currency to maintain market share with a corresponding erosion in dollar revenues and profit margins. At the same time, the dollar cost of American labor remained the same or rose in line with U.S. inflation. The combination of lower dollar revenues and unchanged or higher dollar costs resulted in severe hardship for those U.S. companies selling abroad. Similarly, U.S. manufacturers competing domestically with imports whose dollar prices were declining saw both their profit margins and sales volumes reduced. The shoe is now on the other foot, as Japanese firms attempt to cope with a yen that appreciated by more than 100 percent in real terms between 1985 and 1988.

In general, a change in the real exchange rate should lead to changes in the price of imports relative to the price of domestically sourced goods, thereby benefiting some sectors of the economy and adversely affecting others. Real long-run exchange risk, then, is largely the risk associated with relative price changes that are brought about by currency changes. Such relative price changes are most likely to occur when a government intervenes to control prices and/or wages. For example, devaluations are sometimes preceded by and are often followed by price controls. These controls can benefit an MNC that has a subsidiary producing locally for export; the cost of wages and other local inputs remains largely unchanged while the devaluation makes exports more competitive, or even allows the subsidiary to raise prices abroad. By contrast, a subsidiary with extensive domestic sales will likely be hurt by price controls. For instance, within two months following the August 1977 Mexican peso devaluation, automakers' costs went up 50 percent but Mexican authorities only permitted them to raise prices by 10 percent.

To summarize, the economic impact of a currency change on a firm depends on whether it is fully offset by the difference in inflation rates or whether (because of a shift in monetary policy or some other reason) the currency change results in relative price changes; that is, the impact depends on whether the real exchange rate changes. It is these relative price changes that ultimately have the most severe consequences for the firm's long-run exposure.

A less-than-obvious point is that a firm may face more exchange risk if nominal exchange rates do *not* change. Consider, for example, a Brazilian shoe manufacturer producing for export to the United States and Europe. Given Brazil's typically high rate of inflation, if the Brazilian cruzado's exchange rate remains fixed, then its real rate will rise accordingly, and so will the manufacturer's dollar cost of production. Therefore, unless the cruzado devalues, the Brazilian exporter will be placed at a competitive disadvantage to producers located in countries such as Taiwan and South Korea, where costs are rising less rapidly.

Illustration

A particularly dramatic illustration of the effects of a fixed nominal exchange rate combined with high domestic inflation is provided by the unfortunate example of Chile. As part of its plan to bring down the rate of Chilean inflation, the government fixed the exchange rate at 39 pesos to the U.S. dollar in the middle of 1979. Over the next two and one-half years, the Chilean price level rose 60 percent, while U.S. prices rose by only about 30 percent. Thus, by early 1982, the Chilean peso had appreciated in real terms by approximately 23 percent ($1.6/1.3 - 1$) against the U.S. dollar.

An 18 percent "corrective" devaluation was enacted in June 1982, but it was too late. The artificially high peso had already done its double damage to the Chilean economy: It made Chile's manufactured products more expensive abroad, pricing many of them out of international trade; and it made imports cheaper, undercutting Chilean domestic industries. The effects of the overvalued peso were devastating. Banks became insolvent, factories and copper smelters were thrown into bankruptcy, copper mines were closed, construction projects were shut down, and farms were put on the auction block. Unemployment approached 25 percent and some areas of Chile came to resemble industrial graveyards.

An Operational Measure of Exchange Risk

Determining a firm's true economic exposure to exchange risk is a daunting task. It requires a singular ability to forecast the amounts and exchange rate sensitivities of future cash flows. Most firms that follow the economic approach to managing exposure, therefore, must settle for a measure of their economic exposure and resulting exchange risk that is often supported by nothing more substantial than intuition.

Fortunately, there is a workable approach to determining a firm's true economic exposure and susceptibility to exchange risk that avoids the problem of using seat-of-the-pants estimates.[8] The technique is straightforward to apply, requiring only historical data from the firm's actual operations or, in the case of a start-up venture, data from a comparable business.

The approach is based on the notion that it is possible to measure the exchange risk faced by a parent or one of its foreign affiliates by the extent to which variations in the dollar value of the unit's cash flows are correlated with variations in the nominal exchange rate. This is precisely what a regression analysis seeks to establish. A simple and straightforward way to implement this measure, therefore, is to regress actual cash flows from past periods, converted into their dollar values, on the average exchange rate during the corresponding period. Specifically, this involves running the regression

$$CF_t = \alpha + \beta EXCH_t + u_t \tag{1}$$

where CF_t is the dollar value of total affiliate (parent) cash flows in period t, $EXCH_t$ is the average nominal exchange rate (dollar value of one unit of the foreign currency) during period t, and u_t is a random error term with mean 0.

The output from such a regression includes three key parameters: (1) the foreign exchange beta (β) coefficient, which measures the sensitivity of dollar cash flows to exchange rate changes; (2) the t-statistic, which measures the statistical significance of the beta coefficient; and (3) the R^2, which measures the fraction of cash flow variability explained by variation in the exchange rate. The higher the beta coefficient, the greater the impact of a given exchange rate change on the dollar value of cash flows.

Conversely, the lower the beta coefficient, the less exposed the firm is to exchange rate changes. A larger *t*-statistic means a higher level of confidence in the value of the beta coefficient.

But even if a firm has a large and statistically significant beta coefficient, and thus faces real exchange risk, this does not necessarily mean that currency fluctuations are an important determinant of overall firm risk. What really matters is the percentage of total corporate cash flow variability that is due to these currency fluctuations. Thus, the most important parameter, in terms of its impact on the firm's exposure management policy, may well be the regression's R^2. For example, if exchange rate changes explain only 1 percent of total cash flow variability, the firm should not devote much in the way of resources to foreign exchange risk management, even if the beta coefficient is large and statistically significant.

Multiperiod Exposure

The regression represented by Equation (1) is limited by its implicit assumption that an exchange rate change will affect only current period cash flows. In reality, a given exchange rate could affect both current and future cash flows; i.e., current cash flows might be affected by both the current exchange rate and past exchange rates. This suggests using a modified version of Equation (1) or

$$CF_t = \alpha + \beta_1 EXCH_t + \beta_2 EXCH_{t-1} + \cdots$$
$$+ \beta_{n+1} EXCH_{t-n} + u_t \qquad (2)$$

where $EXCH_{t-j}$ is the average exchange rate during period t-j.

How far back one should go in terms of estimating exposure using Equation (2) depends on the particular circumstances facing the firm (e.g., on how free the firm is to change its prices) but as a general rule one year would seem to be sufficient. Beyond this point, prices appear to adjust so as to offset the effects of a currency change. But it is not necessary to trust judgment; one advantage of the regression technique is that one can experiment by including additional periods in the regression to see just how persistent the effects of past currency changes have been.

Limitations

This method is valid only if the sensitivity of future cash flows to exchange rate changes is similar to their historical sensitivity. In the absence of contrary information, this seems to be a reasonable assumption. If the firm has reason to believe that this historical relationship will not persist, however, it must modify its implementation of this method. For example, the nominal foreign currency tax shield provided by a foreign affiliate's depreciation is fully exposed to the effects of currency fluctuations. If the amount of depreciation in the future is expected to differ significantly from its historical values, the effect of the depreciation tax shield should be removed from the cash flows used in the regression analysis and treated separately. Similarly, if the firm has recently entered into a large purchase or sales contract that is fixed in terms of the foreign currency, it might consider the resulting transaction exposure apart from its operating exposure.

The Hedging Decision

The preceding analysis implies that real economic exposure to exchange risk occurs under two general sets of circumstances:

1. Some cash flows are fixed in foreign currency terms.
2. Exchange rate changes cause relative price changes.

Of the two sources of risk, the second is the more significant. For one thing, in countries with high and variable inflation, fixed currency contracts are avoided as a matter of course. Second, most of the month-to-month variation in exchange rates is unrelated to differential inflation rates. On the basis of a detailed study of twenty-three pairs of countries, Richard Roll reported that less than 10 percent of the monthly variation in any exchange rate can be attributed to inflation.[9] The 10 percent figure, furthermore, is for pairs of countries such as the United States and Argentina, where the annual inflation differential is close to 100 percent. For pairs such as the United States and Germany, where the inflation differential is small, inflation typically accounts for less than 2 percent of the monthly variation in exchange rates. In other words, there is a very strong relationship between exchange rate changes and relative price changes. Although Roll's work does not allow him to determine whether exchange rate changes cause relative price changes or vice versa, it seems clear that currency appreciations or depreciations are likely to affect relative prices—at least in the short run.

Applying the theory of exchange risk to the individual firm requires a forecast of the relationship between exchange rates, relative prices, and the company's real cash flows. This can be obtained by using regression analysis, as suggested previously, or by constructing, and then analyzing in depth, a set of plausible scenarios. Given a forecast of the future relation between real cash flows and exchange rates, management must then decide whether to hedge or take other action to reduce exchange risk. *Hedging* a particular currency exposure involves establishing an offsetting currency position such that whatever is lost or gained on the original currency exposure is exactly offset by a corresponding foreign exchange gain or loss on the currency hedge.

The firm can use a variety of hedging techniques, but before using them it must first decide what its hedging objective is, and how much of its exposure to hedge. In addition, how should exchange rate considerations be incorporated into operating decisions that will affect the firm's exchange risk posture? These and other issues are dealt with here. But before discussing these points, it is worthwhile to first introduce the hedging techniques available to manage transaction exposure, since this is the type of exposure with which most protective measures were designed to cope.

Hedging Techniques

Earlier, it was noted that a transaction exposure arises whenever a company is committed to a foreign currency-denominated transaction. Since the transaction will result in a future foreign currency cash inflow or outflow, any change in the exchange rate between the time the transaction is entered into and the time it is settled in cash will lead to a change in the dollar (home currency) amount of the cash inflow or outflow. Protective measures to guard against transaction exposure include using forward contracts, price adjustment clauses, or currency options, and borrowing or lending in the foreign currency. Alternatively, the company could try to invoice all transactions in dollars and so avoid transaction exposure entirely. However, eliminating transaction exposure does not mean eliminating all foreign exchange risk. The residual exposure—

longer-term operating exposure—still remains; its management is discussed in the next section in this chapter.

The various techniques for managing transaction exposure can be illustrated by examining the case of General Electric's deutsche mark exposure. Suppose that on January 1, GE is awarded a contract to supply turbine blades to Lufthansa, the West German airline. On December 31 of that year, GE will receive payment of DM 25 million for these blades. The most direct way for GE to hedge this receivable is to sell a DM 25 million forward contract for delivery in one year. Alternatively, it can use a money market hedge, which would involve borrowing DM 25 million for one year, converting it into dollars, and investing the proceeds in a security that matures on December 31. As we shall see, if interest rate parity holds, both methods will yield the same results. Other approaches to managing its transaction exposure include risk shifting, risk sharing, exposure netting, and buying a current option.

Forward Market Hedge

By selling forward the proceeds from its sale of turbine blades, GE can effectively transform the currency denomination of its DM 25 million receivable from deutsche marks to dollars, thereby eliminating all currency risk on the sale. To see this, suppose the current spot price for the deutsche mark is DM 1 = $0.40, while the one-year forward rate is DM 1 = $0.3828. Then, a forward sale of DM 25 million for delivery in one year will yield GE $9,570,000 on December 31. Table 2–2 shows the cash flow consequences of combining the forward sale with the deutsche mark receivable, given three possible exchange rate scenarios.

Table 2–2. Possible Outcomes of Forward Market Hedge on December 31

Spot Exchange Rate (12/31)	Value of Original Receivable (12/31) (1)	+	Gain (Loss) on Forward Contract (2)	=	Total Cash Flow (12/31) (3)
DM 1 = $0.40	$10,000,000		($430,000)		$9,570,000
DM 1 = $0.3828	$9,570,000		0		$9,570,000
DM 1 = $0.36	$9,000,000		$570,000		$9,570,000

Regardless of what happens to the future spot rate, Table 2–2 demonstrates that GE still gets to collect $9,570,000 on its turbine sale. Any exchange gain or loss on the forward contract will be offset by a corresponding exchange loss or gain on the receivable. Table 2–2 also shows that the true cost of hedging cannot be calculated in advance since it depends on the future spot rate, which is unknown at the time the company enters into the forward contract. In the example above, the actual cost of hedging can vary between +$430,000 and −$570,000, where a "+" represents a cost and a "−" represents a negative cost or a gain. In percentage terms, the cost varies between −5.7 percent and +4.3 percent.

This points out the distinction between the traditional method of calculating the annualized cost of a forward contract and the correct method, which measures its opportunity cost. Specifically, the cost of a forward contract is usually measured as its annualized forward discount or premium; or

$$\frac{360}{n} \frac{(e_0 - f_1)}{e_0}$$

where e_0 is the current spot rate (dollar price) of the foreign currency, f_1 is the forward rate, and n is the length, in days, of the forward contract. In GE's case, this cost would equal 4.3 percent.

But this approach is wrong because the relevant comparison must be between the dollars per unit of foreign currency (FC) received with hedging, f_1, and the dollars received in the absence of hedging, e_1, where e_1 is the future (unknown) spot rate on the date of settlement; that is, the real cost of hedging is an opportunity cost. In particular, if the forward contract had not been entered into, the future value of each unit of foreign currency would have been e_1 dollars. Thus, the true annualized dollar cost of the forward contract per dollar's worth of foreign currency sold forward equals

$$\frac{360}{n} \frac{(e_1 - f_1)}{e_0}$$

In fact, in an efficient market, the *expected* cost (value) of a forward contract must be zero. Otherwise, there would be an arbitrage opportunity. Suppose, for example, that General Electric management believes that despite a one-year forward rate of $0.3828, the deutsche mark will actually be worth about $0.3910 on December 31. Then GE could profit by buying (rather than selling) deutsche marks forward for one year at $0.3828 and, on December 31, completing the contract by selling deutsche marks on the spot market at $0.3910. If GE is correct, it will earn $0.0082 (0.392 − 0.3828) per deutsche mark sold forward. On a DM 25 million forward contract, this would amount to $205,000, a substantial reward for a few minutes of work.

The prospect of such rewards would not go unrecognized for long, which is why the forward rate is likely to be an unbiased estimate of the future spot rate. Therefore, unless GE or any other company has some special information about the future spot rate that it has *good* reason to believe is not adequately reflected in the forward rate, it should accept the forward rate's predictive validity as a working hypothesis and avoid speculative activities. After the fact, of course, the actual cost or value of a forward contract will turn out to be positive or negative (unless the future spot rate equals the forward rate), but this feature cannot be predicted in advance.

Money Market Hedge

Suppose deutsche mark and U.S. dollar interest rates are 15 percent and 10 percent, respectively. Using a money market hedge, General Electric will borrow DM 25/1.15 million = DM 21.74 million for one year, convert it into $8.7 million in the spot market, and invest the $8.7 million for one year. On December 31, GE will receive 1.10 x $8.7 million = $9.57 million from its dollar investment. GE will use these dollars to pay back the 1.1 × DM 21.74 million = DM 25 million it owes in principal and interest. As Table 2–3 shows, the exchange gain or loss on the borrowing and lending transactions exactly offsets the dollar loss or gain on GE's deutsche mark receivable.

The gain or loss on the money market hedge can be calculated simply by subtracting the cost of repaying the deutsche mark debt from the dollar value of the investment. For example, in the case of an end-of-year spot rate of $0.40, the DM 25 million in principal and interest will cost $10 million to repay. The return on the dollar investment is only $9.57 million, leaving a loss of $430,000.

Table 2–3. Possible Outcomes of Money Market Hedge on December 31

Spot Exchange Rate (12/31)	Value of Original Receivable (12/31) (1)	+	Gain (Loss) on Money Market Hedge (2)	=	Total Cash Flow (12/31) (3)
DM 1 = $0.40	$10,000,000		($430,000)		$9,570,000
DM 1 = $0.3828	$9,570,000		0		$9,570,000
DM 1 = $0.36	$9,000,000		$570,000		$9,570,000

The fact that the net cash flows from the forward market and money market hedges are identical is not coincidental. The interest rates and forward and spot rates were selected so that interest rate parity holds. In effect, the simultaneous borrowing and lending transactions associated with a money market hedge enable the firm to create a "homemade" forward contract. The effective rate on this forward contract will equal the actual forward rate if interest rate parity holds. Otherwise, a covered interest arbitrage opportunity would exist.

Risk Shifting

General Electric could have avoided its transaction exposure altogether if Lufthansa had allowed it to price the sale of turbine blades in dollars. Dollar invoicing, however, does not eliminate currency risk; it simply shifts that risk from GE to Lufthansa (which now has dollar exposure), which may or may not be better able or more willing to bear it. Despite the fact that this form of risk shifting is a zero-sum game, it is common in international business as firms typically attempt to invoice exports in strong currencies and imports in weak currencies.

For example, a sharp decline in the value of the dollar during 1977 led many Japanese, West German, and Swiss exporters to demand payment in their own currencies. Similarly, U.S. exporters began pricing in dollars following the rise in the U.S. dollar's value in the early 1980s. However, valuable sales may be forgone by limiting contract terms to the home currency. Flexibility in the choice of currencies for sales as well as for purchases gives a firm added bargaining power to extract price concessions or enables it to expand its sales. The increased profit generated from these added sales can more than offset the potential exchange losses involved.

Is it possible to gain from risk shifting? Not if one is dealing with informed customers or suppliers. To see why, consider the GE-Lufthansa deal. If Lufthansa is willing to be invoiced in dollars for the turbine blades, that must be because Lufthansa calculates that its deutsche mark equivalent cost will be no higher than the DM 25 million price it was originally prepared to pay. Since Lufthansa does not have to pay for the turbine blades until December 31, its cost will be based on the spot price of the dollars as of that date. By buying dollars forward at the one-year forward rate of DM 1 = $0.3828, Lufthansa can convert a dollar price of P into a deutsche mark cost of $P/0.3828$. Thus, the maximum dollar price, P_M, Lufthansa should be willing to pay for the turbine blades is the solution to

$$P_M/0.3828 = 25,000,000$$

or $P_M = \$9,570,000$.

Considering that GE can guarantee itself $9.57 million by pricing in deutsche marks and selling the resulting DM 25 million forward, it will certainly not accept a lower dollar price than this above figure. The bottom line is that both Lufthansa and General Electric will be indifferent between the choice of a U.S. dollar price or a deutsche mark price only if the two prices are equal at the forward exchange rate. Therefore, since the deutsche mark price arrived at through arm's length negotiations is DM 25 million, the dollar price that is equally acceptable to Lufthansa and GE can only be $9.57 million. Otherwise, this would mean that one or both of the parties involved in the negotiations has ignored the possibility of currency changes. Such naivete is unlikely to exist for long in the highly competitive world of international business.

Pricing Decisions

Notwithstanding the view expressed above, top management has sometimes failed to take into account anticipated exchange rate changes in making operating decisions and has left financial managers with the essentially impossible task, through purely financial operations, of seeking to recover a loss that is already incurred at the time of the initial transaction. To illustrate this, suppose that GE has priced Lufthansa's order of turbine blades at $10 million and then, because Lufthansa demands to be quoted a price in deutsche marks, converts the dollar price to a deutsche mark quote of DM 25 million, using the spot rate of DM 1 = $0.40.

In reality, the quote is worth only $9.57 million, even though it is booked at $10 million, since that is the risk-free price that GE can guarantee for itself by using the forward market. If GE management wanted to sell the blades for $10 million, it should have set a deutsche mark price equal to DM 10,000,000/0.3828 = DM 26.12 million. Thus, GE lost $430,000 the moment it signed the contract (assuming that Lufthansa would have agreed to the higher price rather than turn to another supplier). This loss is not an exchange loss; it is a loss due to management inattentiveness.

The general rule on credit sales overseas is to convert between the foreign currency price and the dollar price using the forward, not the spot, rate. If the dollar price is high enough, the exporter should follow through with the sale. Similarly, if the dollar price on a foreign currency-denominated import is low enough, the importer should follow through on the purchase. All this rule does is to recognize that a deutsche mark (or any other foreign currency) tomorrow is not the same as a deutsche mark today. This is the international analogue to the insight that a dollar tomorrow is not the same as a dollar today.

In the case of a sequence of payments to be received at several points in time, the foreign currency price should be a weighted average of the forward rates for delivery on those dates.

Exposure Netting

Exposure netting involves offsetting exposures in one currency with exposures in the same or another currency, where exchange rates are expected to move in such a way that losses (gains) on the first exposed position should be offset by gains (losses) on the second currency exposure. This is a portfolio approach to hedging, since it recognizes that the total variability or risk of a currency exposure portfolio should be less than the sum of the individual variabilities of each currency exposure considered in isolation. The assumption underlying exposure netting is that the net gain or loss on the entire currency exposure portfolio is what matters rather than the gain or loss on any individual monetary unit.

It is easy to see, for example, that a DM 1 million receivable and DM 1 million payable cancel each other out, with no net (before-tax) exposure. It may be less obvious that such exposure netting can be accomplished using positions in different currencies. But companies practice multicurrency exposure netting all the time.

In practice, exposure netting involves one of three possibilities: (1) a firm can offset a long position in a currency with a short position in that same currency; (2) if the exchange rate movements of two currencies are highly, positively correlated (e.g., the Swiss franc and deutsche mark), then the firm can offset a long position in one currency with a short position in the other; and (3) if the currency movements are negatively correlated (e.g., the French franc and deutsche mark), then short (or long) positions can be used to offset each other.

Currency Risk Sharing

In addition to or instead of a traditional hedge, General Electric and Lufthansa can agree to share the currency risks associated with their turbine blade contract. They can do this by developing a customized hedge contract imbedded in the underlying trade transaction. For example, the base price could be set at DM 25 million, but the parties would share the currency risk beyond a specific neutral zone. The neutral zone represents the currency range in which risk is not shared.

Suppose the neutral zone is specified as a band of exchange rates: $0.39 − 0.41:DM 1, with a base rate of DM 1 = $0.40. This means that the exchange rate can fall as far as $0.39:DM 1 or rise as high as $0.41:DM 1 without reopening the contract. Within the neutral zone, Lufthansa must pay GE the dollar equivalent of DM 25 million at the base rate of $0.40, or $10 million. Thus, Lufthansa's cost can vary from DM 24.39 million to DM 25.64 million ($10,000,000/0.41 to $10,000,000/0.39). But if the DM depreciates from $0.40 to, say, $0.35, the actual rate will have moved $0.04 beyond the lower boundary of the neutral zone ($0.39:DM 1). This amount is shared equally. Thus, the exchange rate actually used in settling the transaction is $0.38:DM 1 ($0.40 − 0.04/2). The new price of the turbine blades becomes DM 25,000,000 x 0.38, or $9.5 million. Lufthansa's cost rises to DM 27.14 million (9,500,000/0.35). In the absence of a risk-sharing agreement, the contract value to GE would have been $8.75 million. Of course, if the deutsche mark appreciates beyond the upper bound to, say, $0.45, GE does not get the full benefit of the DM's rise in value. Instead, the new contract exchange rate becomes $0.42 ($0.40 + 0.04/2). GE collects DM 25,000,000 × 0.42 or $10.5 million, while Lufthansa pays a price of DM 23.33 million ($10,500,000/0.45).

Figure 2–4 compares the currency risk protection features of the currency risk-sharing arrangement with that of a traditional forward contract (at a forward rate of $0.3828) and a no-hedge alternative. Within the neutral zone, the dollar value of GE's contract under the risk-sharing agreement stays at $10 million. This is equivalent to Lufthansa selling GE a forward contract at the current spot rate of $0.40. Beyond the neutral zone, the contract's dollar value rises or falls only half as much under the risk-sharing agreement as under the no-hedge alternative. The value of the hedged contract remains the same, regardless of the exchange rate.

Although a currency risk-sharing agreement for a one-time transaction has been illustrated, such agreements are typically used only by companies involved in long-term export/import contracts. Currency-risk sharing agreements reduce both the frequency of contract revisions and the impact of currency fluctuations on profits. They help companies avoid two pricing extremes: adjusting prices continuously as exchange rates move, or holding the price constant so that one party has a price fixed in its home currency while the other party either has windfall profits or suffers a drastic loss in profit margin or market share.[10]

Foreign Currency Options

Thus far, we have examined how firms can hedge known foreign currency transaction exposures. Yet, in many circumstances, the firm is uncertain whether the hedged foreign currency cash inflow or outflow will materialize. In the previous section,

Figure 2–4. Currency Risk Sharing

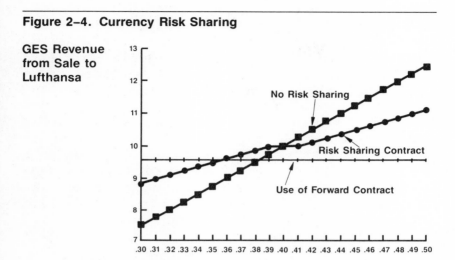

GES Revenue from Sale to Lufthansa

GE learned on January 1 that it had won a contract to supply turbine blades to Lufthansa. But suppose that, while GE's bid on the contract was submitted on January 1, the winning bid would not be announced until April 1. Hence, during the three-month period from January 1 to April 1, GE does not know whether it will receive a payment of DM 25 million on December 31. This uncertainty has important consequences for the appropriate hedging strategy.

GE would like to guarantee that the exchange rate does not move against it between the time it bids and the time it gets paid, should it win the contract. The danger of not hedging is that its bid will be selected and the deutsche mark will decline in value, possibly wiping out GE's anticipated profit margin. For example, if the forward rate on April 1 for delivery December 31 falls to DM 1 = $0.36, the value of the contract will drop by $570,000, from $9.57 million to $9 million.

The apparent solution is for GE to sell the anticipated DM 25 million receivable forward on January 1. But if GE does that, and loses the bid on the contract, it still has to sell the currency, which it will have to get by buying on the open market, perhaps at a big loss. For example, suppose the forward rate on April 1 for December 31 delivery has risen to $0.4008. To eliminate all currency risk on its original forward contract, GE would have to buy DM 25 million forward at a price of $0.4008. The result would be a loss of $450,000 [(0.3828 − 0.4008) × 25,000,000] on the forward contract entered into on January 1 at a rate of $0.3828.

Until recently, GE or any company that bid on a foreign contract in a foreign currency and was not assured of success would be unable to resolve its foreign exchange risk dilemma. The advent of currency options has changed all that. Specifically, the solution to managing its currency risk in this case is for GE, at the time of its bid, to purchase an option to sell DM 25 million on December 31. For example, suppose that on January 1, GE can buy, for $100,000, the right to sell Citibank DM 25 million on December 31 at a price of $0.3828 per deutsche mark. If it enters into this option contract with Citibank, GE will guarantee itself a minimum price ($9.57 million) should its bid be selected, while simultaneously ensuring that if it lost the bid, its loss would be limited to the price paid for the option contract (the premium of $100,000). Should the spot price of the deutsche mark on December 31 exceed $0.3828, GE would let its option contract expire unexercised and convert the DM 25 million at the prevailing spot rate.

There are two types of options available to manage exchange risk. A *put option*, such as the one appropriate to GE's situation, gives the buyer the right, but not the obligation, to sell a specified number of foreign currency units to the option seller at a fixed dollar price, up to the option's expiration date. Alternatively, a *call option* is the right, but not the obligation, to buy the foreign currency at a specified dollar price, up to the expiration date.

A call option is valuable, for example, when a firm has offered to buy some foreign asset, such as another firm, at a fixed foreign currency price but is uncertain whether its bid will be accepted. By buying a call option on the foreign currency, the firm can lock in a maximum dollar price for its tender offer, while at the same time limiting its downside risk to the call premium in the event its bid is rejected.

Currency options are a valuable risk management tool in other situations as well. Conventional transaction exposure management says to wait until sales are booked or orders placed before hedging them. But if a company does that, it faces potential losses from exchange rate movements. That is because the foreign currency-denominated price does not necessarily adjust right away to changes in the value of the dollar. As a matter of policy, to avoid confusing customers and salespeople, most companies do not change their price list every time the exchange rate changes. Unless and until the foreign currency price changes, the unhedged company may suffer a decrease in its profit margin. Because of the uncertainty of anticipated sales or purchases, however, forward contracts are an imperfect tool to hedge the exposure.

For example, a company that commits to a foreign currency price list for, say, three months has a foreign currency exposure that depends on the unknown volume of sales at those prices during this period. Thus, the company does not know what volume of forward contracts to enter into to protect its profit margin on these sales. For the price of the premium, currency options allow the company to insure its profit margin against adverse movements in the foreign currency while guaranteeing fixed prices to foreign customers. Without options, the firm might be forced to raise its foreign currency prices sooner than the competitive situation warranted.

A company can also use currency options to hedge its exposure to shifts in a competitor's currency. Companies competing with firms from other nations may find their products at a price disadvantage if a major competitor's currency weakens, allowing the competitor to reduce its prices. Thus, the company will be exposed to fluctuations in the competitor's currency even if it has no sales in that currency. For example, a Swiss engine manufacturer selling in West Germany will be placed at a competitive disadvantage if dollar depreciation allows its principal competitor, located in the United States, to sell at a lower price in West Germany. Purchasing out-of-the-money put options on the dollar and selling them for a profit if they move into the money (which will happen if the dollar depreciates enough) will allow the Swiss firm to partly compensate for its lost competitiveness. Because the exposure is not contractually set, forward contracts are again not as useful as options in this situation.

Forward contracts are ideally used when the exposure has a straight risk-reward profile: Forward contract gains or losses are exactly offset by losses or gains on the underlying transaction. But if the transaction exposure is uncertain because the volume and/or the foreign currency prices of the items being bought or sold are unknown, a forward contract will not match it. By contrast, currency options are a good hedging tool in situations where the quantity of foreign exchange to be received or paid out is uncertain.

The general rules to follow in choosing between currency options and forward contracts for hedging purposes can be summarized as follows:[11]

1. When the quantity of a foreign currency cash outflow is known, buy the currency forward; when the quantity is unknown, buy a call option on the currency.
2. When the quantity of a foreign currency cash inflow is known, sell the currency forward; when the quantity is unknown, buy a put option on the currency.
3. When the quantity of a foreign currency cash flow is partially known and partially uncertain, use a forward contract to hedge the known portion and an option to hedge the maximum value of the uncertain remainder.

These rules presume that the financial manager's objective is to reduce risk, and not to speculate on the direction or volatility of future currency movements. They also presume that both forward and options contracts are fairly priced. In an efficient market, the expected value or cost of either of these contracts should be zero. Any other result would introduce the possibility of arbitrage profits. The presence of such profits would attract arbitrageurs as surely as bees are attracted to honey. Their subsequent attempts to profit from inappropriate prices will return these prices to their equilibrium values.

The Value of Hedging

Many firms follow a selective hedging policy designed to protect against anticipated currency movements. But if financial markets are efficient, firms cannot hedge against *expected* exchange rate changes. This statement just means that interest and forward rates and sales contract prices are assumed to reflect currency changes that are already anticipated, thereby offsetting the loss-reducing benefits of hedging with higher costs. In the case of Mexico, for instance, the one-year forward discount in the futures market was close to 100 percent just before the peso was floated in 1982. The unavoidable conclusion is that a firm can protect itself only against *unexpected* currency changes; however, these changes are unpredictable by definition, and consequently impossible for a company to profit from them. Firms can use hedging to reduce the riskiness of their cash flows, which—as seen in Chapter 1—may increase their expected cash flows by reducing the costs of financial distress. (Such a hedging objective is discussed in the next section of this chapter.)

Other standard techniques for responding to anticipated currency changes, including the ones just discussed, are summarized in Figure 2–5. But such techniques are vastly overrated in terms of their profit potential. If a devaluation is unlikely, they are costly and inefficient ways of doing business. If a devaluation is expected, as in the case of Mexico in 1982, the cost of using the techniques, such as the cost of local borrowing, rises to reflect the anticipated devaluation. Just prior to the Mexican devaluation, for example, every company in Mexico was trying to delay peso payments. Of course, this cannot produce a net gain because one company's payable is another company's receivable. Moreover, if one company wants peso trade credit, another must offer it. Assuming that both the borrower and the lender are rational, a deal will not be struck until the interest cost rises to reflect the expected decline in the peso.

A company can earn excess returns from the above techniques only to the extent that it can estimate the probability and timing of a devaluation with greater accuracy than the general market. Attempting to profit from foreign exchange forecasting, however, is speculating, not hedging. The hedger is well advised to assume that the market knows as much as the hedger. Those who feel that they have superior information will choose to speculate, but this activity should not be confused with hedging. The real value to a firm of factoring currency change expectations into its pricing and credit decisions is to prevent others from profiting at its expense.

Figure 2–5. Basic Hedging Techniques

Depreciation	Appreciation
Sell local currency forward	Buy local currency foward
Reduce levels of local currency cash and marketable securities	Increase levels of local currency cash and marketable securities
Tighten credit (reduce local currency receivables)	Releax local currency credit terms
Delay collection of hard currency receivables	Speed up collection of soft currency receivables
Increase imports of hard currency goods	Reduce imports of soft currency goods
Borrow locally	Reduce local borrowing
Delay payment of account payable	Speed up payment of accounts payable
Speed up dividend and fee remittances to parent and other subsidiaries	Delay dividend and fee remittances to parent and other subsidiaries
Speed up payment of intersubsidiary accounts payable	Delay payment of intersubsidiary account payable
Delay collection of intersubsidiary account receivable	Speed up collection of intersubsidiary accounts receivable
Invoice exports in foreign currency and imports in local currency	Invoice exports in local currency and imports in foreign currency

Source: Alan C. Shapiro, *Multinational Financial Management,* 2nd edition (Needham, Mass.: Allyn and Bacon, 1986), p. 210.

Under some circumstances, a company can benefit at the expense of the local government without speculating. This would involve the judicious use of market imperfections and/or existing tax asymmetries. In the case of an overvalued currency, such as the Mexican peso in 1982, if exchange controls are not imposed to prevent capital outflows and hard currency can be acquired at the official exchange rate, then money can be moved out of the country via intercompany payments. For instance, a subsidiary can speed payment of intercompany accounts payable, make immediate purchases from other subsidiaries, or speed remittances to the parent company. Unfortunately, governments are not unaware of these tactics. During a currency crisis, when hard currency is scarce, the local government can be expected to block such transfers, or at least to raise their cost.

There may be other advantages to hedging aside from risk reduction. If forward contract losses are treated as a cost of doing business, while gains are taxed at a lower capital gains rate, the firm can engage in tax arbitrage. It is evident under this circumstance that even if the before-tax cost of a forward contract is zero, the after-tax value of the contract will be positive. The presence of such a tax arbitrage situation means that the financial manager does not have to beat the market to come out ahead. In the absence of financial market imperfections or tax asymmetries, however, the net expected value of hedging over time should be zero.

Hedging Objectives

Management's decision about the specific hedging tactics and strategy to pursue will be determined largely by its objectives. These objectives, in turn, should reflect management's view of the world, particularly its beliefs about how markets work. Before setting its own hedging objectives, management should ask itself the key question posed by Gunter Dufey: "Could we profitably exist as a purely financial institution?"[12] Honest introspection would reveal that most companies earn their "keep" because of their superior marketing, production, organization, and technical skills. There are two principal implications of this doctrine of "comparative advantage" for exchange risk management:

1. The principal exposure management goal of financial executives should be to arrange their firm's financial affairs in such a way as to minimize the real (as opposed to accounting) effects of exchange rate changes, subject to the costs of such rearrangements.
2. The major burden of exchange risk management must fall on the shoulders of marketing and production executives. They deal in imperfect product and factor markets where their specialized knowledge provides them with a real advantage; that is, they should be able to consistently outperform their competitors in the markets in which they operate because of their superior knowledge.

Managing Exchange Risk

As seen earlier, in order for a currency depreciation or appreciation to significantly affect a firm's value, it must lead to changes in the relative prices either of the firm's inputs, or of the products sold in various countries. The impact of these currency-induced relative price changes on corporate revenues and costs depends on the extent of the firm's commitment to international business as well as its degree of operational flexibility. To the extent that exchange rate changes do bring about relative price changes, the firm's competitive situation will be altered. As a result, management may wish to adjust its production process or its marketing mix to accommodate the new set of relative prices. Conceptually, this is no different from an adjustment to changing relative prices within a country—for example, adjustment for higher energy costs.

By making the necessary marketing and production revisions, the firm can either counteract the harmful effects of, or capitalize on the opportunities presented by, a currency appreciation or depreciation. The following are some of the proactive marketing and production strategies that a firm can pursue in response to anticipated or actual real exchange rate changes and their associated relative price changes.

Proactive Marketing and Production Strategies

Marketing initiatives	Production initiatives
Market selection	Product sourcing
Product strategy	Input mix
Pricing strategy	Plant location
Promotional options	

The appropriate response to an anticipated or actual real exchange rate change depends, crucially, on the length of time that real change is expected to persist. For example, following a real home currency appreciation, the exporter has to decide whether and how much to raise its foreign currency prices. If the change were expected to be temporary, and if regaining market share would be expensive, the exporter would probably prefer to maintain its foreign currency prices at existing levels. While this would mean a temporary reduction in unit profitability, the alternative—raising prices now and reducing them later when the real exchange rate declined—might be even more costly. A longer-lasting change in the real exchange rate, however, probably would lead the firm to raise its foreign currency prices at the expense of losing some export sales. Assuming a still more permanent shift, management might choose to build production facilities overseas. Alternatively, if the cost of regaining market share were sufficiently great, the firm could hold foreign currency prices constant, counting on shifting production overseas to preserve its longer-term profitability.

A general rule of thumb is that movements in the real exchange rate toward equilibrium are likely to be longer lasting than real exchange rate movements away from equilibrium. For example, the 1982 Mexican peso devaluation reduced the deviation from PPP that then existed. This movement towards equilibrium indicated that the real value of the peso likely would remain at its depressed level for the foreseeable future. Alternatively, the prior increase in the real value of the Mexican peso, because of a fixed nominal exchange rate combined with a high rate of Mexican inflation, widened the peso's deviation from PPP. This disequilibrium situation signaled the likelihood of a real peso devaluation in the not-too-distant future.

Aside from watching for the deviation from the PPP rate, the most important factor that determines whether a particular exchange rate change is a movement toward or away from equilibrium is the extent of government involvement in the currency change. In a freely floating exchange rate system, the general presumption is that any exchange rate change is a movement toward equilibrium. Many speculators, for example, got "burned" during the early 1980s by constantly betting that the dollar would decline in value, the assumption being that it was overvalued. In an efficient market, however, the real value of an asset such as the dollar should follow a random walk, being just as likely to increase in value (as the dollar subsequently did) as to decrease in value (which it did still later).

A real exchange rate change resulting from government intervention, however, should be treated as a movement away from equilibrium that therefore is likely to be temporary only. On the other hand, a change in the real exchange rate brought about by a cessation of government intervention should be considered a shift toward equilibrium.

To summarize this section, managers trying to cope with actual or anticipated exchange rate changes must first determine whether the exchange rate change is real or nominal. If real, the manager must then assess the permanence of the change. In general, real exchange rate movements that narrow the gap between the current rate and the equilibrium rate are likely to be longer lasting than are those that widen the gap. Neither, however, will be permanent. Rather, in a world without an anchor for currency values, there will be a sequence of equilibrium rates, each of which has its own implications for the marketing and production strategies discussed in the next two sections of this chapter.

Marketing Management of Exchange Risk

One of the international marketing manager's tasks should be to identify the likely effects of an exchange rate change and then act on them by adjusting pricing, product, credit, and market selection policies. Unfortunately, multinational marketing executives generally have ignored exchange risk management. Marketing programs are almost always "adjusted" only *after* changes in exchange rates. Yet the design of a firm's marketing strategy under conditions of home currency fluctuation presents considerable opportunity for gain of competitive leverage.[13] To clarify matters, the currency appreciations or depreciations referred to in these sections all involve changes in the real, not just the nominal, exchange rate.

Market Selection

Major strategic questions for an exporter involve the markets in which to sell and the relative marketing support to devote to each market. From an exposure point of view, a key consideration is the impact of currency changes on the revenue to be gained from future sales in individual countries. Marketing management must take into account its company's economic exposure and selectively adjust the marketing support, on a nation-by-nation basis, to maximize long-term profit. As a result of the strong dollar, some discouraged U.S. firms actually pulled out of markets made unprofitable by foreign competition.

It also is necessary to consider the issue of market segmentation within individual countries. A firm that sells differentiated products to more affluent customers may not be harmed as much by a foreign currency devaluation as might be a mass marketer. On the other hand, following a depreciation of the home currency, a firm that sells primarily to upper income groups may find it is now able to penetrate mass markets abroad.

Market selection and market segmentation provide the basic parameters within which a company may adjust its marketing mix over time. In the short term, however, neither of these two basic strategic choices can be altered in reaction to actual or anticipated currency changes. Instead, the firm must select certain tactical responses such as adjustment of pricing, promotional, and credit policies. In the long run, if the real exchange rate change persists, the firm will have to revise its marketing strategy.

Pricing Strategy

A firm selling overseas should follow the standard economic proposition of setting the price that maximizes dollar (home currency, or HC) profits (by equating marginal revenues and marginal costs). In making this determination, however, profits should be translated using the forward exchange rate that reflects the true expected dollar (HC) value of the receipts upon collection.

In the wake of a foreign currency devaluation, a firm selling in that market should consider opportunities to increase the foreign currency prices of its products. The problem, of course, is that producers in the country whose currency has devalued now will have a competitive cost advantage. They can use that advantage to expand their market share by maintaining, or only increasing slightly, their local currency prices. In any event, the existence of local competitors will limit an exporter's ability to recoup dollar profits by raising foreign currency selling prices.

At best, therefore, an exporter will be able to raise its product prices by the extent of the devaluation. At worst, in an extremely competitive situation, the exporter will be forced to absorb a reduction in home currency revenues equal to the percentage decline in the exchange rate. In the most likely case, foreign currency prices can be raised somewhat and the exporter will make up the difference through a lower profit margin on its foreign sales.

Under conditions of a real home currency devaluation, it follows that exports will gain a competitive price advantage on the world market. However, a company does not have to reduce export prices by the full amount of the devaluation. Instead, it has the options either of increasing unit profitability (price skimming) or of expanding its market share (penetration pricing). The decision is influenced by such factors as whether this change is likely to persist, economies of scale, the cost structure of expanding output, consumer price sensitivity, and the likelihood of attracting competition if high unit profitability is obvious.

The greater the price elasticity of demand, the greater the incentive to hold down price and thereby expand sales and revenues. Similarly, if significant economies of scale exist, generally it will be worthwhile to hold down price and expand demand, thereby lowering unit production costs. The reverse is true if economies of scale are nonexistent or if price elasticity is low.

Historically, many of the exports of U.S. multinationals appear to have fit the latter category (low price elasticity of demand) because they were technologically innovative or differentiated, often without close substitutes. Research by Raymond Vernon on American MNCs, for example, stresses the role of innovation (especially labor-saving innovation) in the expansion of international trade by the United States, as well as the relative price insensitivity for such innovation.[14] This is one reason why there was a pronounced tendency for American firms not to cut prices after the real dollar devaluations of the 1970s.

Similarly, following dollar appreciation in the early 1980s, European and Japanese automakers were able to keep the dollar prices up on their car exports to the United States. European cars figure largely in the luxury car market, which is fairly insensitive to price swings. And import quotas enabled the Japanese car companies to avoid the price cutting they find necessary in their highly competitive home market. This factor, combined with the strong dollar, resulted in the major Japanese automakers earning about 80 percent of their 1984 worldwide profits in the United States.

By the late 1980s, however, the United States was no longer the across-the-board leader in the development and application of new technology to manufactured goods. As the U.S. technological edge has eroded, more American companies have faced competition from companies in other industrial nations. Absent other strategies to reduce costs or the price sensitivity of demand, these American firms have become more subject to exchange risk.

Turning now to domestic pricing after devaluation, a domestic firm facing strong import competition may have much greater latitude in pricing. It has the choice of potentially raising prices consistent with import price increases, or of holding prices constant in order to improve market share. Again, the strategy depends on such variables as economies of scale and consumer price sensitivity.

In 1978, for instance, General Motors and Ford Motor Company took advantage of price increases on competitive foreign autos to raise prices on their Chevette and Pinto models. The prices of those small cars previously had been held down, and even reduced, in an attempt to combat the growing market share of West German and Japanese imports. However, the declining value of the U.S. dollar relative to the deutsche mark and yen led the West German and Japanese automakers to raise their dollar prices. The price increases by the American manufacturers, which were less than the sharp rise in import prices, improved profit margins while keeping the domestic cars competitive with their foreign rivals.

Of course, if a firm selling in the domestic market is operating with weak or nonexistent import competition, it will have minimal ability to adjust its prices following devaluation. This is a common situation confronting those MNCs with subsidiaries operating in countries that severely restrict imports, such as Mexico. To improve both its competitive position vis-a-vis other domestic producers and its dollar profit margins, the Mexican affiliate would have to substitute local for imported materials and services.

In deciding how to respond to a home currency appreciation, firms that fail to price competitively must consider not just sales that will be lost today but also the likelihood of losing future sales as well. The reason is that once they build market share, foreign firms are unlikely to pull back. For example, foreign capital goods manufacturers used the period when they had a price advantage to build strong U.S. distribution and service networks. U.S. firms that had not previously bought foreign-made equipment became loyal customers. When the dollar fell, foreign firms opened U.S. plants to supply their distribution systems and hold onto their customers.

The same is true in many other markets as well; a customer who is lost may be lost forever. Americans who discover California wines may not switch back to French wines even after a franc devaluation. Similarly, in the auto business, a customer who is satisfied with a foreign model may stick with that brand for a long time.

Advance planning in pricing is particularly important if price controls are expected to follow a devaluation. For example, the U.S. government imposed a price freeze along with the August 1971 devaluation of the dollar. Foreign firms are especially susceptible to such controls because they face subtle pressures to be "good corporate citizens" and not skirt the intent of the law.

Several options are available to a firm to counteract expected controls. One possibility is to set prices at an artificially high level and accept the resulting loss of market share. If devaluation occurs and price controls are imposed, the firm is then in a better position to continue operating profitably, even with the inevitable rise in costs.

An alternative approach is to raise list prices but continue selling at existing prices—in effect, to sell at a discount. This mitigates the problem of competing with higher prices before a devaluation or a similar change (such as increased inflation) in the pricing environment. The effect of price controls can be eluded by eliminating part or all of the discount.

Another common means of circumventing price controls is to develop new products that are only slightly altered versions of the firm's existing goods, and then sell them at higher prices. This method is particularly convenient for a multinational company already dealing in a range of differentiated products with a continual stream of updated or new merchandise.

Such anticipatory or "proactive" planning is especially important for firms that are heavy users of imported materials. Companies unable to raise their prices when production costs increase will have the unpleasant choices of producing inferior merchandise, cutting back on service, sustaining considerable losses, or dropping unprofitable product lines.

Promotional Strategy

Promotional strategy similarly should take into account anticipated exchange rate changes. A key issue in any marketing program is the size of the promotional budget for advertising, personal selling, and merchandising. *Promotional decisions* should build in exchange rates explicitly, especially in allocating budgets among countries. The appreciation of the U.S. dollar in the early 1980s illustrates these promotional considerations. For example, European countries, with their lower costs and comparable Alpine skiing, attempted to capitalize on those factors with campaigns aimed at wooing American skiers from the Rocky Mountains. Success is evident in the fact that despite record snowfalls in the Rockies in 1984, many American skiers decided on Alpine ski vacations instead. And rather than taking ski equipment, a number of them decided to buy skis, boots, and sweaters overseas as well.

Again, the firm's proper objective is to maximize the present value of future profits, not the appearance of its balance sheet. It is important to make promotional commitments for more than a one-year planning horizon, because advertising, for example, generally requires cumulative expenditures over time in order to build and maintain a viable brand franchise.

A firm exporting its products after a domestic devaluation may well find that the return per dollar expenditure on advertising or selling is increased as a function of the product's improved price positioning. The exporter also may find it has improved its ability to sell the product based on the option of greater distribution margins or consumer dealing. Devaluation may well be the time to reevaluate the mix of advertising, personal selling, and merchandising because the firm has more market leverage. A foreign currency devaluation, on the other hand, is likely to reduce the return on marketing expenditures, thereby requiring a more fundamental shift in the firm's product policy.

Product Strategy

Exchange rate fluctuations may affect the timing of the introduction of new products. In periods of currency uncertainty, distributors may be reluctant to accept new product introduction risks involving up-front investment in marketing costs, especially for inventories and advertising. The firm must devise a strategy for new product introduction and market selection as a function of its relative exposure in different markets. Because of the competitive price advantage, the period after a home currency devaluation or foreign currency revaluation may be the ideal time to develop a brand franchise.

Similarly, *product deletion decisions,* as products become obsolete or fall into consumer disfavor, may be influenced by exchange risk considerations. Indeed, companies may continue manufacturing marginally profitable goods at home if a home currency devaluation is expected. Conversely, they might stop producing those goods if a home currency revaluation or foreign currency devaluation is likely.

Exchange rate fluctuations also affect *product line decisions.* As in the case of market segmentation, it follows that a firm pursuing foreign markets after a home currency devaluation potentially will be able to expand its product line and reach a wider spectrum of consumers in the foreign market. Following devaluation, a domestic firm facing import competition in its local market may have the option to emphasize and place greater marketing support behind the top of its line (which generally has a higher margin), because it will be at a competitive price advantage.

Following a foreign currency devaluation or home currency revaluation, a firm may have to reorient its product line completely and target it to a higher-income, more quality-conscious, less price-sensitive constituency. Volkswagen, for example, achieved its export prominence on the basis of low-priced, stripped-down, low-maintenance cars. Its product line was limited essentially to one model: the relatively unchanging "Bug," or Beetle model. The appreciation of the deutsche mark relative to the dollar in the early 1970s, however, effectively ended Volkswagen's ability to compete primarily on the basis of price. The company lost over $310 million in 1974 alone attempting to maintain its market share by lowering deutsche mark prices.

To compete in the long run, Volkswagen was forced to revise its product line and sell relatively high-priced cars from an extended product line to middle income consumers on the basis of quality and styling rather than cost.

The equivalent strategy for firms selling to the industrial, rather than consumer, market and confronting a strong home currency is *product innovation,* financed by an expanded research and development budget. Kollmorgen Corporation, a Connecticut-based electronic components company responded to the strong dollar, in part, by increasing its research and development budget by 40 percent.

Production Management of Exchange Risk

The adjustments discussed so far involve attempts to alter the dollar value of foreign currency revenues. Forward-looking exchange risk management also should consider the possibility of changing the firm's production and product sourcing strategies to reduce its dollar costs.

Consider, for example, the possible responses of U.S. firms to a strong dollar. The basic strategy would involve shifting the firm's manufacturing base overseas. Such a shift, however, can be accomplished in more than one way. A shutdown of capacity in the United States effectively does the job, but there are less draconian approaches.

Input Mix

Outright additions to facilities overseas naturally accomplish a manufacturing shift. A more flexible solution is increased purchasing of components overseas. In a survey of 152 manufacturing companies, the Machinery and Allied Products Institute found that 77 percent of them had increased their global sourcing since the rise of the dollar.[15]

This input sourcing shift is as it should be. The principal effect of a real exchange rate change is to change the price of domestically produced goods relative to foreign goods. A well-managed firm should be searching constantly for ways to substitute between domestic and imported inputs, depending on the relative prices involved and the degree of substitution possible. This strategy is shown, for example, in Caterpillar Tractor's philosophy of world-wide sourcing: "We're trying to become international in buying as well as selling. We expect our plants, regardless of where they're located, to look on a world-wide basis for sources of supply."[16]

For a firm already manufacturing overseas, the cost savings associated with using a higher proportion of domestically produced goods and services following local currency depreciation will depend on subsequent domestic price behavior. Goods and services used in international trade, or with a high import content, will exhibit greater dollar (HC) price increases than those with a low import content or with little involvement in international trade.

In the long term, when increasing production capacity, the firm should consider the option of designing its new facilities so as to provide added flexibility in making substitutions among various sources of goods. Maxwell House, for instance, can blend the same coffee by using coffee beans from Brazil, the Ivory Coast, and other producers. The extra design and construction costs must, of course, be weighed against the advantages of being able to respond to relative price differences among domestic and imported inputs.

Shifting Production Among Plants

Multinational firms with worldwide production systems can allocate production among their several plants in line with the changing dollar costs of production. The managers of a multinational corporation have the option of increasing production in a nation whose currency has devalued and decreasing production in a country where there has been a revaluation. Contrary to conventional wisdom, therefore, multinational firms may well be subject to less exchange risk than an exporter, given the MNC's greater ability to adjust its production (and marketing) operations on a global basis in line with changing relative production costs.

A good example of this flexibility is provided by Westinghouse Electric Corporation, which began quoting its customers prices on goods from foreign affiliates more often following the increase in the real value of the dollar in the early 1980s: gas turbines from Canada, generators from Spain, circuit breakers and robotics from Britain, and electrical equipment from Brazil. Its sourcing decisions take into account both more favorable exchange rates and subsidized export financing available from foreign governments.

Of course, the theoretical ability to shift production is more limited in reality. The limitations depend on many factors, not the least of which is the power of the local labor unions involved. However, the innovative nature of the typical MNC means a continued generation of new products. The sourcing of those new products, such as General Motors' J-cars, among the firm's various plants certainly can be done with an eye to the costs involved.

A strategy of production shifting presupposes that the MNC has already created a portfolio of plants worldwide. For example, as part of its global sourcing strategy, Caterpillar now has dual sources, domestic and foreign, for some products. These allow the company to "load" the plant that offers the best economies of production, given exchange rates at any moment. These arrangements, however, also create manufacturing redundancies and impede the move to cut costs.

The cost of multiple sourcing is especially great where there are economies of scale, which would ordinarily dictate the establishment of only one or two plants to service the global market. But most firms have found that, in a world of uncertainty, significant benefits may be derived from production diversification. Hence, despite the apparently higher unit costs associated with smaller plants, currency risk may provide one more reason for the use of multiple production facilities.

The case of the auto industry illustrates the potential value of maintaining a globally balanced distribution of production facilities in the face of fluctuating exchange rates. For auto manufacturers in Japan and Sweden, among other countries, with all their production facilities located domestically, it has been feast or famine. When the home currency appreciates, as in the 1970s, the firms' exports suffer from a lack of cost competitiveness. On the other hand, a real depreciation of the home currency, as in the early 1980s, is a time of high profits.

By contrast, Ford and General Motors, with their worldwide manufacturing facilities, have substantial leeway in reallocating various stages of production among their several plants in line with relative production and transportation costs. For example, Ford can shift production among the United States, Spain, West Germany, Great Britain, Brazil, and Mexico.

Plant Location

A firm without foreign facilities that is exporting to a competitive market whose currency has devalued may find that sourcing components abroad is insufficient to maintain unit profitability. Despite its previous hesitancy, the firm may have to locate new plants abroad. In many cases, third country plant locations are a viable alternative, depending especially on the labor intensity of production or the projections for further monetary realignments. Volkswagen, for example, began producing in Brazil before establishing U.S. production facilities.

Before making such a major commitment of its resources, management should attempt to assess the length of time a particular country will retain its cost advantage. If the local inflationary conditions that led to a nominal exchange rate change are expected to persist, a country's apparent cost advantage may soon reverse itself. In Mexico, for example, the wholesale price index rose 18 percent relative to U.S. prices between January 1969 and May 1976. This led to a 20 percent devaluation of the peso in September 1976. Within one month, though, the Mexican government allowed organized labor to raise its wages by 35 percent to 40 percent. As a result, the devaluation's effectiveness was nullified, and the government was forced to devalue the peso again in less than two months. Even then, however, the Mexican government fixed the nominal value of the peso while inflation persisted at a high level.

Cutting Costs Domestically

Many American companies assaulted by foreign competition have made prodigious efforts to improve their U.S. productivity—closing inefficient plants, automating heavily, and negotiating wage and benefit cutbacks and work rule concessions with unions. Many have also started programs to heighten productivity and improve product quality through employee motivation. Although these are all things that should have been done before, it was dollar strength that gave them urgency.

Planning

Thus far, the marketing and production strategies advocated are based on knowledge of exchange rate changes. Even if exchange rate changes are unpredictable, however, contingency plans can be made. The first step is to take several plausible currency scenarios and to analyze the effect on the firm's competitive position under each set of conditions. Using the results of the analysis, the firm should set forth strategies to deal with each of the possibilities. The planning and information gathering required to convert a particular strategy into a course of action would then follow.

Then, if a currency change actually occurs, the firm is able to quickly adjust its marketing and production strategies in line with the plan. It can begin immediately to redirect its marketing efforts toward those markets in which it has become more competitive. It can also begin to shift its production sourcing and input mix in the directions management has determined would be most cost effective under the circumstances. If new plant locations are required, planning in advance reduces the lead time involved in site selection, labor recruitment, and contractor and supplier selection.

Obviously, the range of possible scenarios is infinite and the costs of gathering the required information can be substantial. In selecting scenarios to evaluate, a firm should rank them by probability of occurrence in addition to likely impact. The firm should concentrate its efforts on scenarios that have a high probability of occurrence and that would also strongly affect the firm.

The ability to plan for volatile exchange rates has fundamental implications for exchange risk management because there is no longer such a thing as the "natural" or "equilibrium" rate. Rather, there is a sequence of equilibrium rates, each of which has its own implications for corporate strategy. Success in such an environment—where change is the only constant—depends on a company's ability to react to change within a shorter time horizon than ever before. As they emphasize proactive planning and the development of competitive options such as outsourcing, flexible manufacturing systems, a global network of production facilities, and shorter product cycles, the companies that can succeed within the core economy can do so across a broad range of real exchange rates.

In a volatile world, these investments in flexibility are likely to yield high returns. For example, flexible manufacturing systems permit faster production response times to shifting market demand. Similarly, foreign facilities, even if they are uneconomical at the moment, can pay off by enabling companies to shift production in response to changing exchange rates or other relative cost shocks.

The greatest boost to competitiveness comes from compressing the time it takes to bring new and improved products to market. The edge a company gets from shorter product cycles is dramatic: Not only can it charge a premium price for its exclusive products but also it can incorporate more up-to-date technology in its goods and respond faster to emerging market niches and changes in taste. The ideal often held up is the speedy way that retailers such as The Limited clothiers operate: If they see an item catching on with the public, at their stores or someone else's, they can have it manufactured in quantity and on their shelves within perhaps three weeks.

This is harder to do if a company produces, say, automobiles or heavy machinery. But apparently radical improvements in new product delivery time are within reach even in these industries. In response to the soaring yen, which made their old products less competitive, Japanese automakers are making a frantic effort to squeeze to less than two years (from four years) the time it takes between the initial design and the actual production of a new car. With better planning and more competitive options, corporations can now change their strategies substantially before the impact of any currency change can make itself felt.

As a result, the adjustment period following a large exchange rate change has been compressed dramatically. The 100 percent appreciation of the Japanese yen against the dollar from 1985 to 1988, for example, sparked some changes in corporate strategy that are likely to be long-lasting—increased direct investment in the United States and East Asia by Japanese companies to cope with the high yen and to protect their markets from any trade backlash; upscaling by Japanese manufacturers to reduce the price sensitivity of their products and broaden their markets; massive cost-reduction programs by Japanese plants, with a long-term impact on production technology; and an increase in joint ventures between competitors.

The changes are so profound that some economists and executives are saying the value of the yen is no longer strongly affecting profits at many Japanese companies. Despite the sharp jump in the value of the yen during 1987, manufacturers' pretax profits soared 54 percent in the 1987 third quarter from a year earlier, the largest year-to-year rise in nearly a decade.

Some of this profit improvement was due to the fact that the weak dollar made raw materials, particularly oil, a lot cheaper in terms of the yen. Most important, Japanese companies dealt with the higher yen by cutting costs and increasing productivity sharply. One typical result: Victor Company of Japan, also known as JVC, could sell for ¥130,000 in 1987 a 21-inch television that sold for ¥200,000 in 1985.

An increasingly attractive option is to take the change in the currency markets as given and focus on the new pattern of opportunities and risks. The better prepared that corporations are for constant change, the more they will come to regard exchange rate swings as strategic opportunities rather than mere risks—a chance to get ahead of their more rigid competitors. The emphasis must, therefore, be on developing more competitive options, streamlining their organizations, and emphasizing resilience and adaptability over stability. In a competitive world, a differential capacity to adjust to—and actively shape—changing markets is a key strategic asset.

Financial Management of Exchange Risk

The one attribute that all the strategic marketing and production adjustments have in common is that they take time to accomplish in a cost-effective manner. Otherwise, the firm will incur unreasonable costs. The role of financial management, based on the definition of hedging introduced at the beginning of this section, is to structure the firm's liabilities in such a way that during the time the strategic operational adjustments are underway, the reduction in asset earnings is matched by a corresponding decrease in the cost of servicing these liabilities.

Liability Management

One possibility is to finance the portion of a firm's assets used to create export profits so that any shortfall in operating cash flows resulting from an exchange rate change is offset by a reduction in debt service expenses. For example, a firm that has developed a sizable export market should hold a portion of its liabilities in the currency of that country. The portion to be held in the foreign currency depends on the size of the loss in profitability associated with a given exchange rate change. No more definite recommendations are possible because the currency effects will vary by company.

As a case in point, Volkswagen, to hedge its operating exposure, should have used dollar financing in proportion to its net dollar cash flow from U.S. sales or sold forward the present value of these future net dollar cash flows, or used some combination of the two methods. This strategy would have cushioned the impact of the deutsche mark revaluation that almost brought the company to its knees. But even this strategy would not have provided a perfect hedge. In Volkswagen's case, the development of products aimed at the more income-elastic segment of the market and the shifting of some production facilities to a lower-cost country was probably the best solution.

The implementation of a hedging policy is likely to be quite difficult in practice, if only because the specific cash flow effects of a given currency change are hard to predict. Trained personnel are required to implement and monitor an active hedging program. Consequently, hedging should be undertaken only when the effects of anticipated exchange rate changes are expected to be significant.

The Role of the Financial Manager
The key to effective exposure management is to integrate currency considerations into the general management process. One approach used by a number of multinationals to develop the necessary coordination among executives responsible for different aspects of exchange risk management is to establish a committee concerned with managing foreign currency exposure. Besides financial executives, such committees should—and often do—include the senior officers of the company, such as the vice president-international, top marketing and production executives, the director of corporate planning, and the chief executive officer. The most desirable feature of this arrangement is that top executives are exposed to the problems of currency risk management and then can incorporate exchange rate expectations into particular nonfinancial decisions.

Another way to encourage this process is to hold subsidiary and other operating managers responsible for net operating income targets expressed in the home currency. In this kind of integrated exchange risk program, the role of the financial executive would be three-fold: to provide local operating management with forecasts of inflation and exchange rates; to structure evaluation criteria so that operating managers are not rewarded or penalized for the effects of unanticipated real currency changes; and to estimate and hedge whatever real operating exposure remains after the appropriate marketing and production strategies have been put in place.

3

International Working
Capital Management

The management of working capital in the multinational firm is basically similar to its domestic counterpart. Both are concerned with selecting that combination of current assets—cash, marketable securities, accounts receivable, and inventory—that will maximize the value of the firm. The essential differences between domestic and international working capital management include the impact of currency fluctuations, potential exchange controls, and multiple tax jurisdictions on these decisions, in addition to the wider range of short-term financing and investment opportunities available.

International Cash Management

International money managers attempt to attain, worldwide, the traditional domestic objectives of cash management: (1) to bring the company's cash resources within control as quickly and efficiently as possible, and (2) to achieve the optimum conservation and utilization of these funds. Accomplishing the first goal requires establishing accurate and timely forecasting and reporting systems, improving cash collections and disbursements, and decreasing the cost of moving funds among affiliates. The second objective is achieved by minimizing the required level of cash balances, making money available when and where it is needed, and increasing the risk-adjusted return on those funds that can be invested.

The principles of domestic and international cash management may be identical, but the latter is complicated by its wider scope and the need to recognize the customs and practices of other countries. In the case of moving funds across national borders, a number of external factors inhibit adjustment and constrain the money manager. The most obvious are restrictions that impede the free flow of money into or out of a country. Numerous examples exist, such as former U.S. Office of Foreign Direct Investment (OFDI) restrictions, Germany's Bardepot, and the requirements of many countries that their exporters repatriate the proceeds of foreign sales within a specific period. Although capital controls have become somewhat less prevalent and more relaxed under floating exchange rates, they continue to restrict the free flow of capital and thereby hinder an international cash management program.

There is really only one generalization that can be made about foreign exchange regulations: Controls become more stringent during periods of crisis, precisely when financial managers want to act. Thus, a large premium must be placed on foresight, planning, and anticipation. Aside from a broad statement that borders on being a truism, the basic rule is that government restrictions must be scrutinized on a country-by-country basis to determine realistic options and limits of action.

International cash management includes six key areas: (1) organization, (2) cash planning and budgeting, (3) collecting and disbursing of funds, (4) netting of interaffiliate payments, (5) investing excess funds, and (6) setting an optimal level of worldwide corporate cash balances.

Organization

Compared with a system of granting autonomy to operating units, a fully centralized international cash management program offers a number of advantages:

1. The corporation is able to operate with a smaller amount of cash; pools of excess liquidity are absorbed and

eliminated. Each operation maintains transactions balances only and does not hold speculative or precautionary balances.

2. By reducing total assets, profitability will be enhanced and financing costs reduced.

3. The headquarters staff, with its purview of all corporate activity, can recognize problems and opportunities that an individual unit might not perceive.

4. All decisions can be made using the overall corporate benefit as the criterion.

5. Greater expertise in cash and portfolio management should exist if one group is responsible for these activities.

6. The corporation's total assets at risk in a foreign country can be reduced. Less will be lost in the event of an expropriation or the promulgation of regulations restricting the transfer of funds.

These and other benefits have long been understood by experienced MNCs. Today, the combination of volatile currency and interest rate fluctuations, high real interest rates, and increasingly complex organizations and operating arrangements virtually mandates a highly centralized international cash management system. There is also a trend to place much greater responsibility for cash management in corporate headquarters.

Centralization does not necessarily imply control by headquarters of all facets of cash management. Instead, centralization requires a concentration of decision making at a sufficiently high level within the corporation so that all pertinent information is available readily and can be used to optimize the firm's position.

Cash Planning and Budgeting

Cash receipts and disbursements must be reported and forecast in a comprehensive, accurate, and timely manner. If the headquarters staff is to fully and economically use the company's worldwide cash resources, they must know the financial positions of affiliates, the forecast cash needs or surpluses, the anticipated cash inflows and outflows, local and international money market conditions, and likely movements in currency values.

As a result of rapid and pronounced changes in the international monetary arena, the need for more frequent reports has become acute. Firms that had been content to receive information quarterly now require monthly, weekly, or even daily data. Key figures are often transmitted by telex or telecopier instead of by mail.

Collection and Disbursement of Funds

Accelerating collections both within a foreign country and across borders is a key element of international cash management. Potential benefits exist because long delays often are encountered in collecting receivables, particularly on export sales, and in transferring funds between affiliates and corporate headquarters. Allowing for mail time and bank processing, delays of eight to ten business days are common from the moment an importer pays an invoice to the time when the exporter is credited with funds available for use. Given high interest rates, wide fluctuations in the foreign exchange markets, and the periodic imposition of credit restrictions that have characterized financial markets in recent years, cash in transit has become more expensive and exposed to risk.

With increasing frequency, management at corporate headquarters is participating in the establishment of an affiliate's credit policy, as well as monitoring its collection performance. The principal aims are to minimize float (the transit time of payments), to reduce investment in accounts receivable, and to lower banking fees and other transaction costs. By rapidly converting receivables into cash, a company can increase its portfolio of marketable securities or reduce its borrowing, either earning a higher investment return or saving interest expense.

Whether for national or international collections, accelerating the receipt of funds usually involves: (1) defining and analyzing the different available payment channels, (2) selecting the most efficient method (which can vary by country and customer), and (3) giving specific instructions about procedures to the firm's customers and banks.

In considering payment channels, the full costs of using the various methods must be determined and the inherent delay of each calculated. There are two main periods of delay in the collections process: the time between the dates of customer payment and of receipt and the time for the payment to clear through the banking system. Because banks will be as "inefficient" as possible to increase their float, an MNC cash manager must understand the subtleties of domestic and international money transfers if the firm is to reduce the time funds are held and extract the maximum value from its banking relationships. A number of multinational banks, particularly U.S. banks, offer consulting services to corporations on accelerating collections and using funds within a country, as well as the transnational movement and employment of money. Even sophisticated industrial firms are likely to find these services valuable, particularly when they are applied to collections within a country.

Turning to international cash movements, having all affiliates transfer funds by telex enables the corporation to plan better because the vagaries of mail time are eliminated. Third parties, too, are asked to use wire transfers. To cope with the transmittal delays associated with checks or drafts, customers are instructed in some cases to remit to *mobilization points*, which are centrally located in important regions with large sales volumes. For example, all European customers may be told to make all payments to Switzerland, where the corporation maintains a staff specializing in cash and portfolio management and collections. The funds are managed centrally or are transmitted to the selling subsidiary. A variation is to intercept all collections within a country and then forward them to a central corporate point. Intracountry collection methods vary, but they usually are constrained by prevailing trade customs.

Sometimes customers are asked to pay directly into a designated account at a branch of the bank that is mobilizing the MNC's funds internationally. This approach is particularly useful when banks have large branch networks. Another technique that is used internationally as well as domestically is to have customers remit funds to a designated *lock box*, which is a postal box in the company's name. A local bank or branch of a multinational bank collects and opens the mail received at the lock box one or more times daily. Any deposit or transfer made is immediately reported to the national or regional mobilization office. Credit for the funds is then given to the company, usually on the same day. The period spent in transit thereby can be reduced from up to a week to one or two days.

To reduce clearing time, some companies will set up accounts in its customers' banks, a useful device if there are only a few large customers or where the check clearing time is quite lengthy. Some firms have gone one step further, directly debiting their customers. In *direct debiting*, or preauthorized payment, the customer allows its account to be charged periodically by the supplier or the supplier's bank up to a maximum amount. With this method, there is no customer payment delay, intentional or inadvertent, and mail delay is eliminated. Clearing time also can be reduced by initiating the debit process the correct number of days before the due date.

For disbursements, most European banks operate on a *debit transfer* basis, whereby the customer's account is charged immediately, giving the bank, as opposed to the payer, the advantage of the float. By contrast, U.S. banks operate on a *credit transfer* basis, granting the payer the benefit of the float until the check clears. Furthermore, on international transactions, European banks will debit a company's account two days before foreign funds are made available. American banks, though, will usually provide a firm with *value compensation*; that is, the firm does not give up domestic funds until the foreign funds are provided.

Netting Interaffiliate Payments

Many MNCs engage in a highly coordinated international interchange of material, parts, subassemblies, and finished products among their various units. The importance of these physical flows to the international financial executive is that they are accompanied by a heavy volume of interaffiliate fund flows. Of particular importance is the fact that there is a measurable cost associated with these cross-border fund transfers, including the cost of purchasing foreign exchange (the foreign exchange spread), the opportunity cost of float, and other transaction costs such as cable charges. Thus, there is a clear incentive to minimize the total volume of intracorporate fund flows. This can be achieved by payments netting.

The idea behind a netting system is very simple. Payments between affiliates go back and forth, but only a netted amount need be transferred. For example, if Affiliate A sells goods worth $1 million to Affiliate B, and B in turn sells goods worth $2 million to A, the combined flows total $3 million. On a net basis, however, A need only remit $1 million to B. This type of bilateral netting obviously is only valuable if subsidiaries sell back and forth to each other.

Bilateral netting would be of little use where there is a more complex structure of internal sales. For example, if Subsidiary A sells $1 million worth of goods to Subsidiary B, which in turn sells $1 million worth of goods to Subsidiary C, while C has $1 million in sales to A, bilateral netting would be of no use. But since each affiliate's inflows equal its outflows, on a multilateral basis total transfers would net out to zero.[1]

Essential to any netting scheme is a centralized control point that can collect and record detailed information on the intracorporate accounts of each participating affiliate at specified time intervals. The control point will use a matrix of payables and receivables to determine the net payer or creditor position of each affiliate at the date of clearing.

The costs involved in netting are both explicit and implicit. The explicit continuing costs are those related to the additional management time and expanded communications necessitated by the central clearing system. It should be possible, given the present financial control system, to evaluate the additional resources required for the clearing scheme. There are also costs of a more implicit nature, those related to the behavioral problems resulting from more centralized control. While affiliates might resent the tighter control necessary, such attitudes can be overcome with skill and tact.

Optimal Worldwide Cash Levels

Centralized cash management typically involves the transfer of an affiliate's cash in excess of minimal operating requirements into a centrally managed account, or *pool*. Some firms have established a special corporate entity that collects and disburses funds through a single bank account.

With cash pooling, each affiliate holds locally only the minimum cash balance required for transaction purposes. All precautionary balances are held by the parent or in the pool. As long as the demands for cash by the various units are reasonably independent of each other, centralized cash management can provide an equivalent degree of protection with a lower level of cash reserves.

Investing Excess Funds

A major task of international cash management is to determine the levels and currency denominations of the multinational group's investment in cash balances and money market instruments. Firms with seasonal or cyclical cash flows have special problems such as arranging investment maturities to coincide with projected needs.

To manage this investment properly requires a forecast of future cash needs based on the company's current budget and past experience as well as an estimate of a minimum cash position for the coming period. These projections should take into account the effects of inflation and anticipated currency changes on future cash flows.

Common sense guidelines for managing the marketable securities portfolio globally include:

1. The instruments in the portfolio should be diversified to minimize the risk for a given level of return or to maximize the yield for a given level of risk. Government securities should not be used exclusively. Eurodollar and other instruments may be nearly as safe.
2. The portfolio must be reviewed daily to decide which securities are to be liquidated and particular new investments to be made.
3. In revising the portfolio, care should be taken to ensure that the incremental interest earned more than compensates for added costs such as clerical work, the income lost between investments, fixed charges such as the foreign exchange spread, and commissions on the sale and purchase of securities.

4. If rapid conversion to cash is an important consideration, the marketability (liquidity) of the instrument
   should be carefully evaluated. Ready markets exist for
   some securities, but not for others.
5. The maturity of the investment should be tailored to the
   firm's projected cash needs, or an active secondary
   market should exist.
6. Opportunities for covered or uncovered interest arbitrage
   should be considered carefully.

Accounts Receivable Management

Multinational corporations and domestic firms face the same decisions about the appropriate level of accounts receivable. In the
multinational firm, though, these decisions are complicated by the
existence of different rates of inflation, currency changes, and
restrictions within a market or on currency transfers.

Credit Management

Firms grant trade credit to customers (both domestic and international) because they expect the investment in receivables to be
profitable, because the investment either expands sales volume
or retains sales that otherwise would be lost to competitors. Some
companies also earn a profit on the financing charges they levy
on credit sales.

   The need to scrutinize credit terms is particularly important
in countries experiencing rapid rates of inflation. The incentive
for customers to defer payment, liquidating their debts with less
valuable money in the future, is great. Furthermore, credit standards abroad are often more relaxed than in the home market,
especially in countries lacking alternative sources of credit for small
customers. To remain competitive, MNCs may feel compelled to
loosen their own credit standards. Finally, the compensation system in many companies tends to reward higher sales more than
it penalizes an increased investment in accounts receivable. Local
managers frequently have an incentive to expand sales even if the
corporation overall does not benefit.

Credit Extension

The easier credit terms are, the more sales are likely to be made. But generosity is not always the best policy. The risk of default, increased interest expense on the larger investment in receivables, and the deterioration (through currency devaluation) of the dollar value of accounts receivable denominated in the buyer's currency must be balanced against higher revenues. These additional costs may be partly offset if liberalized credit terms enhance a firm's ability to raise its prices.

Another factor that tends to increase accounts receivable in foreign countries is an uneconomic expansion of local sales, which may occur if managers are credited with dollar sales when accounts receivable are denominated in the local currency (LC). Sales managers should be charged for the expected depreciation in the value of local currency accounts receivable. For instance, if the current exchange rate is LC1 = $0.10, but the expected exchange rate ninety days hence (or the three-month forward rate) is $0.09, managers offering three-month credit terms should be credited with only $0.90 for each dollar in sales booked at the current spot rate.

Whether judging the implications of inflation, devaluation, or both, it must be remembered that when a unit of inventory is sold on credit, a real asset has been transformed into a monetary asset. The opportunity to raise the local currency selling price of the item to maintain its dollar value is lost. This point is obvious but frequently disregarded.

Assuming that both buyer and seller have access to credit at the same cost and reflect, in their decisions, anticipated currency changes and inflation, it normally should make no difference to a potential customer whether he or she receives additional credit or an equivalent cash discount. The MNC may benefit by revising its credit terms, however, in three circumstances:

1. The buyer and seller hold different opinions concerning the future course of inflation or currency changes, leading one of the two to prefer term-price discount trade-offs (i.e., a lower price if paid within a specified period).
2. Because of market imperfections, the MNC has a lower risk-adjusted cost of credit than does its customer. In other words, the buyer's higher financing cost must not be a result of the buyer's greater riskiness.

3. During periods of credit restraint in a country, the affiliate of an MNC may, because of its parent, gain a marketing advantage over its competitors through having access to funds that are not available to local companies. Absolute availability of money, rather than its cost, may be critical.

The following analytical approach enables a firm to compare the expected benefits and costs associated with extending credit internationally. The same analysis also can be used in domestic credit extension decisions, with inflation rather than currency fluctuations being the complicating factor. Let ΔS and ΔC be the incremental dollar sales and costs of goods sold associated with an easing of credit terms. If the expected credit cost per unit of sales revenues, R, is expected to increase to $R + \Delta R$ because of a more lenient credit policy, then terms should be eased if, and only if, incremental profits are greater than incremental credit costs or

$$\Delta S - \Delta C > S\Delta R + \Delta S(R + \Delta R).$$

It should be noted that ΔR reflects forecast changes in currency values as well as the cost of funds over the longer collection period. This analysis can be used to ascertain whether it would be worthwhile to tighten credit, accepting lower sales but at the same time reducing credit costs.

To illustrate the use of this approach, suppose that a subsidiary in France currently has annual sales of $1 million with ninety-day credit terms. It is believed that sales will increase by 6 percent ($60,000) if terms are extended to 120 days. Of these additional sales, the cost of goods sold is $35,000. Monthly credit expenses are 1 percent in financing charges. In addition, a 1.5 percent depreciation of the franc is expected over the next ninety days.

Ignoring currency changes for the moment but considering financing costs, the value today of one dollar of receivables to be collected at the end of ninety days is approximately $0.97. Taking into account the 1.5 percent expected franc devaluation, this value declines to 0.97(1 − 0.015) or $0.955, implying a 4.5 percent cost of carrying French franc receivables for three months. Similarly, one dollar of receivables collected 120 days from now is worth $[1 - (0.01)4][1 - (0.015 + d_4)]$ today or $\$0.945 - 0.96d_4$, where d_4 is the (unknown) amount of currency change during the fourth month. Then, the incremental cost of carrying French franc receivables for the fourth month equals $0.955 - (0.945 - 0.96d_4)$ dollars or $1 + 96d_4$ percent.

Using the formula previously presented,

$$\Delta S - \Delta C = \$25,000$$

$$S\Delta R = \$1,000,000(0.01 + 0.96d_4)$$

$$= \$10,000 + \$960,000d_4 \text{ and}$$

$$\Delta S(R + \Delta R)$$

$$= \$60,000(0.045 + 0.01 + 0.96d_4)$$

$$= \$3,300 + \$57,600d_4.$$

Then, credit extension is worthwhile only if the incremental profit, $25,000, is greater than the incremental cost, $13,300 + $1,017,600d_4$ or

$$d_4 < 11,700/1,017,600 = 1.15 percent.$$

In other words, it is worthwhile providing a fourth month of credit as long as the French franc is expected to devalue by less than 1.15 percent during the fourth month.

One potential problem when evaluating the desirability of extending credit to obtain greater sales is the reaction of competition. It is likely that in an oligopoly, if one firm cuts its effective price by granting longer payment terms, its competitors will be forced to follow, to maintain their market positions. The result could well be no incremental sales and profits for any, but only greater accounts receivable for all.

Inventory Management

Although conceptually the inventory management problems faced by multinational firms are not unique, they may be exaggerated in the case of foreign operations. For instance, MNCs typically have greater difficulty in controlling their overseas inventory and realizing inventory turnover objectives for a variety of reasons, including: long and variable transit times if ocean transportation is used;

lengthy customs proceedings and possibilities of dock strikes; import controls; supply disruption; anticipated changes in currency values; and higher customs duties.

Advance Inventory Purchases

In many developing countries, forward contracts for foreign currency are limited in availability or nonexistent. In addition, restrictions often preclude free remittances, making it difficult if not impossible to convert excess funds into a hard currency. One means of hedging is anticipatory purchases of goods, especially imported items. The trade-off involves owning goods whose local currency prices may rise, which maintains the dollar value of the asset even though inflation and devaluation are virulent, versus forgoing the return on local portfolio investments or not being able to take advantage of potentially favorable fluctuations in the specific prices of these materials. (The attractiveness of holding investments in local-currency money market instruments is frequently overlooked; the after-tax dollar yield, adjusted fully for devaluation, may be positive, sometimes spectacularly so.)

Inventory Stockpiling

The problem of supply failure is of particular importance for any firm dependent upon foreign sources, because of long delivery lead times, the often limited availability of transport for economically sized shipments, and currency restrictions. These conditions may make the knowledge and execution of an optimal stocking policy under a threat of a disruption to supply more critical in the MNC than in the firm that purchases domestically.

The traditional response to such risks has been advance purchases. Holding large quantities of inventory can be quite expensive, though. In fact, the high cost of stockpiling inventory— including financing, insurance, storage, and obsolescence—has led many companies to equate low inventories with effective management. In contrast, production and sales managers typically desire a relatively large inventory, particularly when a cutoff in supply is anticipated.

Some firms do not charge their managers interest on the money tied up in inventory. A danger is that managers in these companies may take advantage of this by stockpiling sufficient quantities of material or goods prior to a potential cutoff, so as to have close to a zero stockout probability. Such a policy, established without regard to the trade-offs involved, can be very costly. The profit performances of those managers who are receiving the benefits of additional inventory on hand should be adjusted to reflect the added costs of stockpiling.

It is obvious that as the probability of disruption increases or as holding costs go down, more inventory should be ordered. Similarly, if the cost of a stockout rises or if future supplies are expected to be more expensive, it will pay to stockpile additional inventory. Conversely, if these parameters move in the opposite direction, less inventory should be stockpiled.

Short-Term Financing

Financing the working capital requirements of a multinational corporation's foreign affiliates poses a complex problem. This complexity stems from the large number of financing options available to the subsidiary of an MNC. Subsidiaries have access to funds from sister affiliates and the parent company, as well as from external sources. This section focuses on developing policies for borrowing from either within or without the corporation when the risk of exchange rate changes is present and different tax rates and regulations are in effect.

Key Factors in Short-Term Financing Strategy

Expected costs and risk, the basic determinants of any funding strategy, are strongly influenced in an international context by six key factors:

1. If forward contracts are unavailable, the crucial issue is whether differences in nominal interest rates among currencies are matched by anticipated exchange rate changes. For example, is the difference between an 8 percent dollar interest rate and a 3 percent Swiss franc interest rate due solely to expectations that the dollar will devalue by 5 percent relative to the franc? The key issue here, in other words, is whether there are deviations from the international Fisher effect. If deviations do exist, then expected dollar borrowing costs will vary by currency, leading to

a decision problem. Trade-offs must then be made between the expected borrowing costs and the exchange risks associated with each financing option.

2. The element of exchange risk is the second key factor. Many firms borrow locally to provide an offsetting liability for their exposed local currency assets. On the other hand, borrowing a foreign currency in which the firm has no exposure will increase the firm's exchange risk. What matters is the covariance between the operating and financing cash flows; that is, the risks associated with borrowing in a specific currency are related to the firm's degree of exposure in that currency.

3. The third essential element is the firm's degree of risk aversion. The more risk averse a firm (or its management), the higher the price it should be willing to pay to reduce its currency exposure. This affects the company's risk-cost trade-off and, consequently, in the absence of forward contracts, influences the selection of currencies it will use to finance its foreign operations.

4. If forward contracts are available, however, currency risk should not be a factor in the firm's borrowing strategy. Instead, relative borrowing costs, calculated on a covered basis, become the sole determinant of the currency or currencies in which to borrow. The key issue here is whether the nominal interest differential equals the forward differential, (i.e., whether interest rate parity holds). If it does hold, then in the absence of tax considerations, the currency denomination of the firm's debt is irrelevant. Covered after-tax costs can differ among currencies because of government capital controls or the threat of such controls. Due to this added element of risk, the annualized forward discount or premium may not offset the difference between the interest rate on the LC loan versus the dollar loan (i.e., interest rate parity will not hold).

5. Even if interest rate parity does hold before tax, the currency denomination of corporate borrowings does matter where tax asymmetries are present. These tax asymmetries are based on the differential treatment of foreign exchange gains and losses on either forward con-

tracts or loan repayments. For example, English companies have a disincentive to borrow in strong currencies because Inland Revenue, the British tax agency, taxes exchange gains on foreign currency borrowings but disallows the deductibility of exchange losses on the same loans. Such tax asymmetries lead to possibilities of borrowing arbitrage, even if interest rate parity holds before tax. The essential point is that, in comparing relative borrowing costs, these costs must be computed on an *after-tax* covered basis.

6. A final factor that may enter into the borrowing decision is political risk. Even if local financing is not the minimum cost option, a number of multinationals will still try to maximize their local borrowings if it is believed that expropriation or exchange controls are serious possibilities. By using local, rather than external, financing, the firm has fewer assets at risk.

Short-Term Financing Objectives

Here are four possible objectives that can guide a firm in deciding where and in which currencies to borrow:[2]

1. *Minimize expected cost.* By ignoring risk, this objective reduces information requirements, allows borrowing options to be evaluated on an individual basis without considering the correlation between loan cash flows and operating cash flows, and lends itself readily to break-even analysis. One problem with this approach is that if risk affects the company's operating cash flows (see Chapter 1), the validity of using expected cost alone is questionable. If forward contracts are available, however, there is a theoretically justifiable reason for ignoring risk; namely, loan costs should be evaluated on a covered (riskless) basis. In that case, minimizing expected cost is the same as minimizing actual cost.

2. *Minimize risk without regard to cost.* If followed to its logical conclusion, this advice would lead a firm to dispose of all its assets and invest the proceeds in government securities; i.e., this objective is impractical and contrary to shareholder interests.

3. *Trade off expected cost and systematic risk.* The advantage of this objective is that, similar to the first objective, it allows a company to evaluate different loans without considering the relationship between loan cash flows and operating cash flows from operations. Moreover, it is consistent with shareholder preferences as described by the capital asset pricing model. In practical terms, however, there is probably little difference between expected borrowing costs adjusted for systematic risk and expected borrowing costs without that adjustment. This is because the correlation between currency fluctuations and a well-diversified portfolio of risky assets is likely to be quite small.

4. *Trade off expected cost and total risk.* The theoretical rationale for this approach was described in Chapter 1. Basically, it relies on the existence of potentially substantial costs of financial distress. On a more practical level, management generally prefers greater stability of cash flows (regardless of investor preferences). Management will typically self-insure against most losses but might decide to use the financial markets to hedge against the risk of large losses. To implement this approach, it is necessary to take into account the covariances between operating and financing cash flows. This approach (trading off expected cost and total risk) is valid only where forward contracts are unavailable. Otherwise, selecting the lowest-cost borrowing option, calculated on a covered after-tax basis, is the only justifiable objective.

Calculating Effective Borrowing Costs

This section presents explicit formulas to compute the effective after-tax dollar costs of local currency financing versus dollar financing.[3] These cost formulas can be used to calculate the cheapest financing source for each future exchange rate. A computer can easily perform this analysis and determine the range of future exchange rates within which each particular financing option is cheapest.

1. *Local currency loan.* In general, the after-tax dollar cost of a local currency loan at an interest rate of r_L by a foreign

affiliate equals the after-tax interest expense less the exchange gain (loss) on principal repayment:

$$interest\ cost\ -\ exchange\ gain\ (loss)$$

$$r_L(1\ -\ d)(1\ -\ t_a)\ -\ d$$

where d is the (expected) LC devaluation, and t_a is the affiliate's effective tax rate. The first term is the after-tax dollar interest cost paid at year-end after an LC devaluation (revaluation) of d; the second is the exchange gain or loss in dollars of repaying a local currency loan valued at one dollar with local currency worth $1 - d$ dollars at the end of the year. The gain or loss has no tax effect for the affiliate because the same amount of local currency was borrowed and repaid.

2. *Dollar loan.* The after-tax cost of a dollar loan is the difference between the after-tax interest expense and the tax deduction (expense) arising from the effect of the currency change on the principal repayment:

$$interest\ cost\ -\ tax\ gain\ (loss)$$

$$r_{US}(1\ -\ t_a)\ -\ dt_a$$

The first term is the after-tax interest expense of borrowing dollars. The second reflects the fact that if the exchange rate fluctuates, the local currency units required to repay a dollar loan will increase (decrease) with a devaluation (revaluation). Depending on the country involved and whether exchange losses or gains on a capital transaction are a taxable event, the affiliate's local tax burden may be smaller or greater.

The break-even rate of currency appreciation or depreciation necessary to equalize the costs of borrowing in the local currency or in the home currency can be found by equating the dollar costs of local currency and parent financing and solving for d:

$$r_{US}(1\ -\ t_a)\ -\ dt_a\ =\ r_L(1\ -\ d)(1\ -\ t_a)\ -\ d$$

or

$$d = \frac{r_L - r_{US}}{(1 + r_L)}.$$

With this break-even analysis, the treasurer can readily see the amount of currency appreciation or depreciation necessary to make one type of borrowing less expensive than another. The treasurer will then compare the firm's actual forecast, determined objectively or subjectively, of currency change with this bench mark.

The logic of this break-even analysis can be extended to other financing alternatives than the two that are presented in this section. In all situations, the cost of each source of funds must be calculated in terms of the relevant parameters (e.g., nominal interest rate, tax rate, future exchange rate) and the expense compared with that of all other possibilities. These calculations and comparisons will differ little from those that are performed here.

Managing Intracorporate Fund Flows

From a financial management standpoint, one of the distinguishing characteristics of the multinational corporation, in contrast to a collection of independent national firms dealing at arm's length with each other, is its ability to move money and profits among its various affiliates through internal transfer mechanisms. These mechanisms, which include transfer prices on goods and services traded internally, intracorporate loans, dividend payments, leading (speeding up) and lagging (slowing down) intracorporate payments, and fee and royalty charges, lead to patterns of profits and movements of funds that would be impossible in the world of Adam Smith.

The ability to adjust intracorporate fund flows and accounting profits on a global basis is potentially of great advantage to the multinational corporation. However, inasmuch as most of the gains derive from the MNC's proficiency at taking advantage of openings in tax laws or regulatory barriers, conflicts between a government and the firm are quite likely.

Financial transactions within the MNC result from the internal transfer of goods, services, technology, and capital. These product and factor flows range from intermediate and finished goods to less tangible items such as management skills, trademarks, and patents. The transactions not liquidated immediately give rise to some type of financial claim such as royalties for the use of a patent or accounts receivable for goods sold on credit. In addition, capital investments lead to future flows of dividends and/or interest and principal repayments. Some of the myriad financial linkages possible in the MNC are depicted in Figure 3–1.

The Nature of the Multinational Financial System

Although the links portrayed in Figure 3-1 can and do exist among independent firms, as pointed out by Donald Lessard[4] and David Rutenberg,[5] the MNC has greater control over the mode and timing of these financial transfers.

Mode of Transfer

The MNC has considerable freedom in selecting the *financial channels* through which funds, allocated profits, or both are moved. For example, patents and trademarks can be sold outright or transferred in return for a contractual stream of royalty payments. By varying the prices at which transactions occur, profits and cash can be shifted within the worldwide organization. Similarly, funds can be moved from one unit to another by adjusting *transfer prices* on intracorporate sales and purchases of goods and services. With regard to *investment flows,* capital can be sent overseas as debt with at least some choice of interest rate, currency of denomination, and repayment schedule, or as equity with returns in the form of dividends. The multinational firm can use these various channels, singly or in combination, to transfer funds internationally, depending on the specific circumstances encountered. Furthermore, within the limits of various national laws and with regard to the relations between a foreign affiliate and its host government, these internal flows may be more advantageous to the MNC than those that would result from dealings with independent firms.

Timing Flexibility

Some internally generated financial claims require a fixed payment schedule; others can be accelerated or delayed. This *leading and lagging* is most often applied to *interaffiliate trade credit,*

Figure 3–1. The Multinational Corporate Financial System

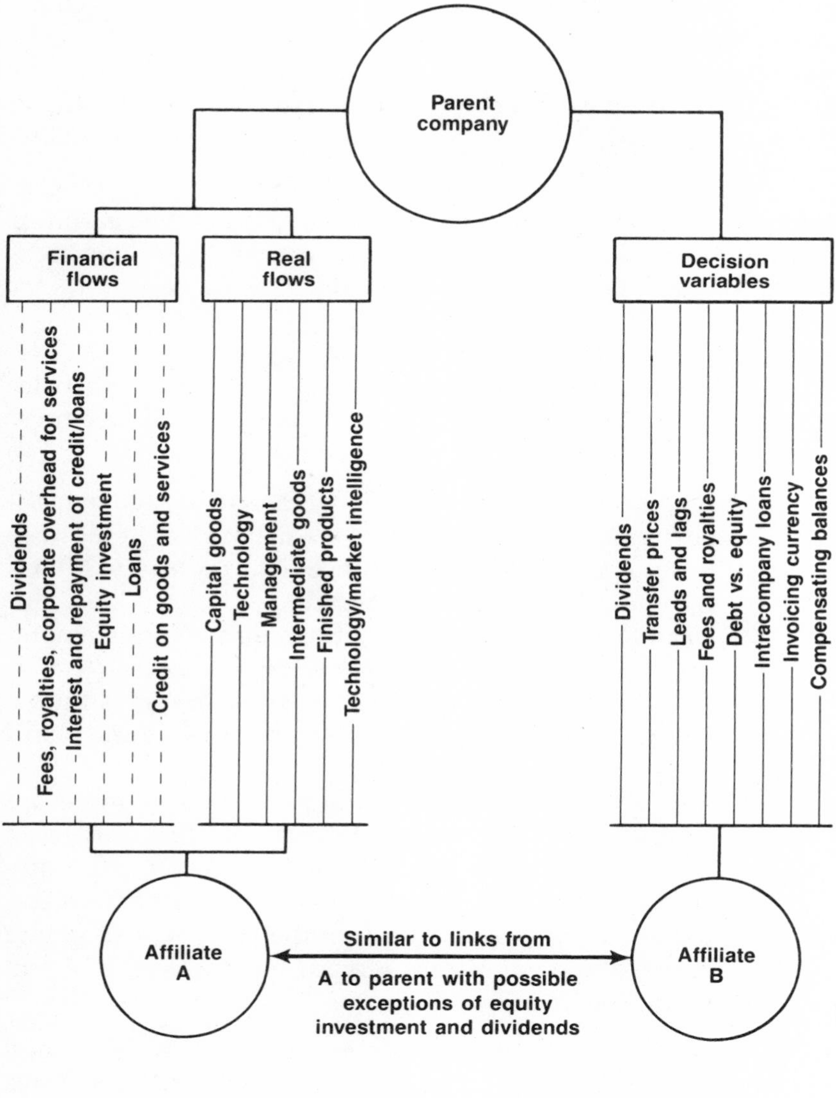

Parent company

Financial flows

Real flows

Decision variables

Dividends
Fees, royalties, corporate overhead for services
Interest and repayment of credit/loans
Equity investment
Loans
Credit on goods and services

Capital goods
Technology
Management
Intermediate goods
Finished products
Technology/market intelligence

Dividends
Transfer prices
Leads and lags
Fees and royalties
Debt vs. equity
Intracompany loans
Invoicing currency
Compensating balances

Affiliate A

Similar to links from A to parent with possible exceptions of equity investment and dividends

Affiliate B

where a change in open account terms from, say, 90 to 180 days, can involve massive shifts in liquidity. (Some nations, both developed and less developed, have regulations concerning the repatriation of the proceeds of export sales. Thus, typically, there is not complete freedom to move funds by leading and lagging.) In addition, the timing of fee and royalty payments may be modified when all parties to the agreement are related. Even if the contract cannot be altered once the parties have agreed, the MNC generally has latitude when the terms are established initially.

In the absence of *exchange controls*, firms have the greatest amount of flexibility in the timing of equity claims. The earnings of a foreign affiliate can be retained or used to pay dividends, which, in turn, can be deferred or paid in advance.

Value of the Multinational Financial System

The ability to transfer funds and to reallocate profits internally presents multinationals with three different types of arbitrage opportunities:[6]

1. *Tax arbitrage.* By shifting profits from units located in high-tax nations to those in lower-tax nations, or from those in a taxpaying position to those with tax losses, MNCs can reduce their tax burden.
2. *Financial market arbitrage.* By transferring funds among units, MNCs may be able to circumvent exchange controls, earn higher risk-adjusted yields on excess funds, reduce their risk-adjusted cost of borrowed funds, and tap previously unavailable capital sources.
3. *Regulatory system arbitrage.* Where subsidiary profits are a function of government regulations (e.g., where a government agency sets allowable prices on the firm's goods) or union pressure, rather than the marketplace, the ability to disguise true profitability by reallocating profits among units may provide the multinational firm with a negotiating advantage.

A fourth possible arbitrage opportunity is the ability to permit an affiliate to negate the effect of credit restraint or controls in its country of operation. If a government limits access to additional borrowing locally, the firm with the ability to draw on external sources of funds not only can achieve greater short-term profits, but it may also be able to attain a more powerful market position over the long term.

Intracorporate Fund Flow Mechanisms

The MNC can be visualized as *unbundling* the total flow of funds between each pair of affiliates into separate components, which are associated with resources transferred in the form of products, capital, services, and technology. For example, dividends, interest, and loan repayments can be matched against capital invested as equity or debt, while fees, royalties, or corporate overhead can be charged for various corporate services, trademarks, or licenses. Transfer prices are charged against product and factor flows.

Transfer Pricing

The pricing of goods and services traded internally is one of the most sensitive of all management subjects, and executives typically are reluctant to discuss it. A government normally presumes that multinationals use transfer pricing to the country's detriment. For this reason, a number of home and host governments have set up policing mechanisms to review the transfer pricing policies of MNCs. The most important uses of transfer pricing include: (1) reducing taxes, (2) reducing tariffs, and (3) avoiding exchange controls.

To illustrate the tax effects associated with changing a transfer price, suppose that Affiliate A is selling 100,000 circuit boards annually to Affiliate B for $10 each. A change in price to $10.50 would simultaneously increase A's income by $50,000 and reduce B's income by the same amount. Assuming that the marginal tax rates on income for A and B are 35 percent and 50 percent, respectively, the transfer price change will increase A's taxes by $17,500 (0.35 × $50,000) and lower B's taxes by $25,000 (0.50 × $50,000) for a net corporate tax saving of $7,500 annually. In effect, profits are being shifted from a higher to a lower tax jurisdiction. In the extreme case, where an affiliate is in a loss position because of high start-up costs, heavy depreciation charges, or substantial investments that are expensed, and that consequently has a zero effective tax rate, profits channeled to that unit can be received tax free.

With respect to tariffs, companies usually set a relatively low price on goods exported to countries with high *ad valorem* duties. This practice enables the purchasing affiliate to price the goods competitively with no loss of revenue to the corporation overall.

Most countries have specific regulations governing transfer prices. For instance, Section 482 of the U.S. Internal Revenue Code calls for *arm's length* prices—prices at which a willing buyer and a willing unrelated seller would freely agree to transact. In light of Section 482, the U.S. government's willingness to use it, and similar authority in most other nations, MNCs today appear to set standard prices for standardized products. However, the innovative nature of the typical multinational ensures a continual stream of new products for which no market equivalent exists. Some flexibility is possible in setting transfer prices. In addition, many of the items traded internally are components and sub-assemblies for which no external market exists. Firms also have latitude in setting prices on rejects, scrap, and returned goods.

Based on their detailed interviews with thirty-nine U.S.-based MNCs, Sidney Robbins and Robert Stobaugh concluded that although tax minimization is a principal goal of transfer pricing, reducing the effect of exchange controls is also quite important.[7] For example, the MNC may raise the intracorporate price for sales to an affiliate with blocked funds, accepting a larger global tax liability in order to access the affiliate's funds. To determine the attractiveness of this step, the manager must know or estimate the effective income tax rates of the selling and purchasing subsidiaries, the probable duration of the blocking, and alternative investment opportunities for the affiliate with the excess funds.

Fees and Royalties

Management services such as headquarters advice, allocated overhead, patents, and trademarks are often unique; therefore, they have no reference market price. The consequent difficulty in pricing these corporate resources makes them suitable for use as additional routes for international fund flows by varying the fees or royalties charged for the use of these intangible factors of production.

Transfer prices for services have the same tax and exchange control effects as do transfer prices on goods, but they often are subject to even greater scrutiny. However, host governments often look with more favor on payments for industrial know-how than for profit remittances. Restrictions that do exist are more likely to be modified to permit a fee for technical knowledge than for dividends.

Leading and Lagging

A highly favored means of shifting liquidity between affiliates is an acceleration or delay (leading and lagging) in the payment of interaffiliate accounts by modifying the credit terms extended by one unit to another. For example, suppose Affiliate A sells $1 million of goods monthly to Affiliate B on 90-day credit terms. On average, A has $3 million of accounts receivable from B, so A is, in effect, financing $3 million of working capital for B. If the terms are changed to 180 days, there will be a one-time shift of an additional $3 million to B. Conversely, a reduction in credit terms to thirty days will involve a flow of $2 million from B to A. This is shown in Table 3–1.

Inasmuch as incremental accounts receivable are financed typically by short-term debt, the costs of leading and lagging are evaluated in the same way as any other use of different sources of borrowing; that is, by considering relevant interest and tax rates and the likelihood of changes in currency values.

The information required to do leading and lagging is similar to that required for netting and international cash management. Thus, the incremental direct costs of running such a system are not great for a firm already centralizing its cash management effort. Problems can arise, however, from the various distortions that these adjustments can cause to affiliate profits and investment bases.

Intracorporate Loans

A principal means of financing foreign operations and moving funds internationally is intracorporate lending activities. The most important intracorporate loan types currently are *direct loans, back-to-back financing, parallel loans,* and *currency swaps.* The first is a straight extension of credit from the parent to an affiliate or from one affiliate to another. The others typically involve an intermediary.

Table 3–1. Fund Transfer Effects of Leading and Lagging

Subsidiary A sells $1,000,000 in goods monthly to subsidiary B

Balance Sheet Accounts	Credit Terms		
	Normal (90 days)	Leading (30 days)	Lagging (180 days)
Subsidiary A			
Accounts receivable from *B*	$3,000,000	$1,000,000	$6,000,000
Subsidiary B			
Accounts payable to *A*	$3,000,000	$1,000,000	$6,000,000
Net Cash Transfers			
From *B* to *A*		$2,000,000	
From *A* to *B*			$3,000,000

Back-to-back loans (also called *fronting loans* or *link financing*) often are employed to finance affiliates located in nations with high interest rates or restricted capital markets, especially when there is a danger of currency controls, or when different rates of withholding tax are applied to loans from a financial institution. In the typical arrangement, the parent company deposits funds with a bank in Country A, which in turn lends the money to a subsidiary in Country B. In effect, a back-to-back loan is an intracorporate loan channeled through a bank. From the bank's point of view, the loan is risk free because it is collateralized fully by the parent's deposit. The bank's role is that of an intermediary or a "front"; compensation is provided by the margin between the interest received from the borrowing unit and the rate paid on the parent's deposit.

A back-to-back loan may offer several potential advantages compared with a direct intracorporate loan. Two of the more important advantages are:

1. Certain countries apply different withholding tax rates to interest paid to a foreign parent and interest paid to a financial institution. A cost saving in the form of lower taxes may be available with a back-to-back loan.
2. If currency controls are imposed, the government usually will permit the local subsidiary to honor the amortization schedule of a loan from a major multinational bank; to stop payment would hurt the nation's credit rating. Conversely, local monetary authorities would have far

fewer reservations about not authorizing the repayment of an intracorporate loan. In general, back-to-back financing provides better protection than does an intracorporate loan against expropriation and/or exchange controls.

A *parallel loan* is a method of effectively repatriating blocked funds (at least for the term of the arrangement), circumventing exchange control restrictions, avoiding a premium exchange rate for investments abroad, or obtaining foreign currency financing at attractive rates. The transaction consists of two related but separate, or parallel, borrowings and usually involves four parties in two different countries. The parent, A, will extend a loan in its home country and currency to a subsidiary of B, whose foreign parent will lend the local currency equivalent in its country to the subsidiary of A. Drawdowns, repayments of principal, and payments of interest are made simultaneously. The differential between the rates of interest on the two loans is determined in theory by the cost of money in each country and anticipated changes in currency values.

A *currency swap* achieves an economic purpose similar to a parallel loan but generally is simpler and involves only two parties and one agreement. Two companies exchange liabilities in two different currencies with each other and undertake to reverse the exchange after a fixed term. Currency swaps are discussed further in Chapter 5.

Dividends
The payment of dividends is by far the most important means of transferring funds from foreign affiliates to the parent company, typically accounting for over 50 percent of all remittances to MNCs in the United States. Among the various factors that multinationals consider when deciding on dividend payments by their affiliates are taxes, financial statement effect, exchange risk, currency controls, financing requirements, availability and cost of funds, and the parent firm's dividend payout ratio. Firms differ, though, in the relative importance they place on these variables, as well as on how systematically they are incorporated into an overall remittance policy.

A major consideration in the dividend decision is the effective tax rate on payments from different affiliates. By varying payout ratios among its foreign subsidiaries, the corporation can reduce its total tax burden. Total tax payments are dependent on the regulations of both the foreign and home nations. The foreign country ordinarily has two types of tax that directly affect tax costs: corporate income taxes and withholding taxes on dividend remittances. In addition, several countries, such as Germany and Austria, tax retained earnings at a higher rate than earnings paid out as dividends. Many nations, such as the United States, tax dividend income received from abroad at the regular corporate tax rate. When this rate is higher than the combined foreign income and withholding taxes, the receipt of dividend income normally will entail an incremental tax cost. A number of countries, including Canada, France, and the Netherlands, do not impose any additional taxes on dividend income from subsidiaries in which the parent holds more than a certain percentage ownership. The United States also taxes certain unremitted profits, known as *Subpart F income*, including dividends paid to holding companies located in tax havens such as Liechenstein and Switzerland.

As an offset to these additional taxes, most countries, including the United States, provide tax credits for taxes already paid by affiliates in countries of operation. For example, if a foreign subsidiary has $100 in pretax income, pays $25 in local income taxes, and a $3 dividend withholding tax and then remits the remaining $72 to its U.S. parent in the form of a dividend, the Internal Revenue Service will impose a $34 tax (0.34 × $100) but will provide a dollar-for-dollar tax credit for the $28 already paid in foreign taxes, leaving the parent with a U.S. tax bill of $6. *Foreign tax credits* from other remittances many be used, in certain cases, to offset these additional taxes. There are also tax treaties between many nations, established to avoid the double taxation of the same income and to provide for reduced dividend withholding taxes.

The policy for dividends from affiliates to the parent is essentially a pure financial decision. The funds remitted must be replaced to leave the affiliate whole. The economic effects of the substitution must be evaluated carefully. Unless constrained, once the firm has decided on the amount of dividends to remit from overseas, it will then withdraw funds from those locations with the lowest overall tax plus other transfer costs.

Currency controls are another major factor in the dividend decision. Nations with balance-of-payments problems are likely to restrict the payment of dividends to foreign companies. These controls vary by country, but generally they limit the size of dividend payments, either in absolute terms or as a percentage of earnings, equity, or registered capital.

Many firms attempt to reduce the danger of such interference by maintaining a record of consistent dividends, designed to show that these payments are part of an established financial program rather than an act of financial speculation against the host nation's currency. Dividends are paid every year, regardless of whether justified by financial and tax considerations, just to demonstrate a continuing policy to the local government and central bank. Even when they cannot be remitted, dividends are sometimes declared for the same reason, namely, to establish grounds for making future payments when these government controls are lifted or modified.

Some companies go further and set a uniform dividend payout ratio throughout the corporate system to establish a global pattern and maintain the principle that affiliates have an obligation to pay dividends to their stockholders. If challenged, the firm can then prove that its French or Brazilian or Italian subsidiaries must pay an equivalent percentage dividend. MNCs often are willing to accept higher tax costs to maintain the principle that dividends are a necessary and legitimate business expense. Many executives believe that a record of consistently paying dividends (or at least declaring them) helps in getting approval for further dividend disbursements.

Debt Versus Equity

Corporate funds invested overseas, whether called debt or equity, require the same rate of return. Nonetheless, MNCs generally prefer to invest in the form of loans rather than equity for several reasons.

First, a firm typically has wider latitude to repatriate funds in the form of interest and loan repayments than as dividends or reductions in equity, because the latter fund flows usually are more closely controlled by governments. A second reason for using intracorporate loans as opposed to equity investments is the possibility of reducing taxes. The likelihood of a tax benefit is due to two factors: (1) interest paid on a loan ordinarily is tax deductible in the host nation, whereas dividend payments are not; and (2) unlike dividends, loan repayments normally do not constitute taxable income to the parent company.

4

Foreign Investment Analysis

The evaluation of foreign investment opportunities is subject to a wider and more complicated set of economic, political, and strategic considerations than those influencing most domestic investment decisions. This complexity and accompanying uncertainty are reflected in the diverse procedures and techniques used by firms to evaluate overseas projects.

Capital Budgeting for the Multinational Corporation

Multinational corporations that evaluate foreign investments find their analyses complicated by several issues that are rarely, if ever, encountered by domestic firms. These issues include how to account for differences between project and parent company cash flows, foreign tax regulations, political risks such as expropriation and currency controls, exchange rate changes and inflation, project-specific financing, and the potential benefits to investors from international diversification.

Alternative Capital Budgeting Frameworks

Once a firm has compiled a list of prospective investments, it must then select from among them the combination of projects that maximizes the company's value to its shareholders. This requires a set of rules and decision criteria that enables managers to determine whether, given an investment opportunity, their firm should accept or reject it.

The Standard Net Present Value Approach

The standard capital budgeting analysis involves first calculating the expected after-tax cash flows associated with a prospective investment, and then discounting those cash flows back to the present using the firm's weighted average cost of capital. If the net present value (NPV) of those cash flows is positive, the investment should be undertaken; if negative, it should be rejected. Formally, the NPV equals

$$NPV = \underset{\substack{\text{Present value} \\ -\text{ of investment} \\ \text{outlay}}}{-I_0} \quad + \underset{\substack{\text{Present value} \\ +\text{ of operating} \\ \text{cash flows}}}{\sum_{t=1}^{n} X_t/(1 + k_0)^t}$$

where

$$NPV = \text{net present value of project}$$
$$I_0 = \text{initial investment}$$
$$X_t = \text{after-tax project cash flow in year } i \text{ if all-equity financed}$$
$$n = \text{anticipated life of the project}$$
$$k_0 = \text{weighted average cost of capital}$$

An Adjusted Present Value Approach

The weighted average cost of capital is simple in concept and easy to apply. A single rate is only appropriate, however, if the financial structures and commercial risks are similar for all investments undertaken. The costs of debt and equity will vary with different project risks. In addition, projects with different risks are likely to possess differing debt capacities, therefore necessitating a separate financial structure for each project. Moreover, the financial package for a foreign investment often includes project-specific loans at concessionary rates or higher cost foreign funds because of home country exchange controls, leading to different component costs of capital.

The weighted average cost of capital figure can, of course, be modified to reflect these deviations from the firm's typical investment. But for some companies, such as those in extractive industries, there is no norm. Project risks and financial structure vary by country, raw material, production stage, and position in the project's life cycle. Such problems can be dealt with by using an alternative procedure, known as the "adjusted present value" (APV) approach.[1] The APV approach involves discounting cash flows at a rate that, by removing the effects of financing, reflects only the project's business risks. This rate, known as the *all-equity* rate, represents the required rate of return on a project financed entirely by equity.

The all-equity rate, k^*, can be used in capital budgeting by viewing the value of a project as the sum of the following components: (1) the present value of project cash flows after taxes but before financing costs, discounted at k^*; (2) the present value of the tax savings on debt financing, discounted at the company's normal domestic borrowing rate, i_d; and (3) the present value of any after-tax savings (penalties) on interest costs associated with project-specific financing, discounted at the before-tax domestic interest rate.[2] This latter differential generally would be due to government regulations and/or subsidies that cause interest rates on restricted funds to diverge from domestic interest payable on unsubsidized, arm's length borrowing.

In equation form, the APV of a project can be expressed as follows:

$$
\begin{array}{cc}
\text{\textit{Present value}} & \text{\textit{Present value}} \qquad (3) \\
- \text{ \textit{of investment}} & + \text{ \textit{of operating}} \\
\text{\textit{outlay}} & \text{\textit{cash flows}}
\end{array}
$$

$$
APV = -I_o \qquad\qquad + \sum_{t=1}^{n} \frac{X_t}{(1 + k)^t}
$$

$$
\begin{array}{cc}
\text{\textit{Present value}} & \text{\textit{Present value}} \\
+ \text{ \textit{of interest}} & + \text{ \textit{of interest}} \\
\text{\textit{tax shield}} & \text{\textit{subsidies}}
\end{array}
$$

$$\$\sum_{t=1}^{n} \frac{T_t}{(1 + i_d)^t} \quad + \sum_{t=1}^{n} \frac{S_t}{(1 + i_d)^t}$$

where

T_t = tax savings in year t due to the specific financing package

S_t = before-tax dollar value of interest subsidies (penalties) in year t due to project specific financing

i_d = before-tax cost of dollar debt

The last two terms in Equation 3 are discounted at the before-tax cost of dollar debt to reflect the relatively certain value of the cash flows due to tax shields and interest savings (penalties).

It should be emphasized that the all-equity cost of capital equals the required rate of return on a *specific* project; i.e., the riskless rate of interest plus an appropriate risk premium based on the project's particular risk. Thus k^* varies according to the risk of the specific project.

According to the capital asset pricing model (CAPM), the market prices only systematic risk relative to the market, rather than total corporate risk. For project analysis, this pricing mechanism means that only the correlation between a project's returns and overall market returns is relevant in determining its required rate of return; interactions of project returns with total corporate returns can be ignored. Thus, each project has its own required return and can be evaluated without regard to the firm's other investments.

Issues in Foreign Investment Analysis

The analysis of a foreign project raises two additional issues:

1. Should cash flows be measured from the viewpoint of the project or the parent?
2. Should the additional economic and political risks that are uniquely foreign be reflected in cash flow or discount rate adjustments?

Parent Versus Project Cash Flows

A substantial difference can exist between the cash flow of a project and the amount that is remitted to the parent firm, because of tax regulations and exchange controls. In addition, many project expenses such as management fees and royalties are revenues to the parent company. Furthermore, the *incremental* revenue contributed by a project to the parent MNC can differ from total project revenues if, for example, the project involves substituting local production for parent company exports or if transfer price adjustments shift profits elsewhere in the system.

Given the differences that are likely to exist between parent and project cash flows, what then are the relevant cash flows to use in evaluating a foreign project? Subsidiary management can be expected, of course, to focus only on those project cash flows that accrue locally. It will tend to ignore the consequences of its investment policies on the economic situation of the rest of the corporation.

Some have suggested that the effect of restrictions on repatriation be ignored. According to economic theory, though, the value of a project is determined by the net present value of future cash flows *back to the investor*. Thus, the parent MNC should value only those cash flows (net of any transfer costs such as taxes) that are or can be repatriated. Only accessible funds can be used to pay dividends and interest, to amortize the firm's debt, and for reinvestment.

To simplify project evaluation, a three-stage analysis is recommended. In the first stage, project cash flows are computed from the subsidiary's standpoint, exactly as if it were a separate national corporation. The perspective would then shift to the parent company. This second stage of analysis requires specific forecasts concerning the amounts, timing, and form of transfers to headquarters. It also involves gathering information about taxes and other expenses that will be incurred in the transfer process. Third and last, the parent company should take into account the indirect benefits and costs, such as an increase or decrease in export sales by another affiliate, that this investment confers on the rest of the system.

Estimating Incremental Project Cash Flows
Essentially, the company must estimate a project's true profitability. "True profitability" is an amorphous concept, but basically

involves determining the marginal revenue and marginal costs associated with the project. In general, incremental cash flows to the parent can be found only by subtracting worldwide parent company cash flows (without the investment) from post-investment parent company cash flows. This entails management performing the following:

1. Adjusting for the effects of transfer pricing and fees and royalties.

   ◆ Use market costs/prices for goods, services, and capital transferred internally.
   ◆ Add back fees and royalties to project cash flows, since they are benefits to the parent.
   ◆ Remove the fixed portions of such costs as corporate overhead.

2. Adjusting for global costs/benefits which are not reflected in the project's financial statements.

   ◆ Cannibalization of sales of other units.
   ◆ Creation of incremental sales by other units.
   ◆ Additional taxes owed when repatriating profits.
   ◆ Foreign tax credits usable elsewhere.
   ◆ Diversification of production facilities.
   ◆ Market diversification.
   ◆ Provision of a key link in a global service network.

The second set of adjustments involves incorporating the project's strategic purpose and its impact on other units. These strategic considerations embody the factors that will be discussed in a following section.

While the principle of valuing and adjusting incremental cash flows is conceptually simple, it can be complicated to apply. Let us look at how this recommended procedure might be applied, with special attention to the tax question.

Incorporating Tax Factors
Because only after-tax cash flows are relevant, it is necessary to determine when, and what, taxes must be paid on foreign-source profits. On the basis of existing tax laws, taxes paid are a function of the time of remittance (are profits remitted immediately or are they reinvested?), the form of remittance (e.g., dividends,

loan repayments, transfer price adjustments), the foreign income tax rate, the existence of withholding taxes, tax treaties between home and host country, and the existence and usability of foreign tax credits.

Because of these complexities in estimating actual after-tax cash flows back to the parent, a simpler approach is recommended for calculating the foreign investment's tax liabilities. This approach makes two conservative assumptions: first, the maximum amount of funds available for remittance in each year actually is remitted; second, the tax rate applied to these cash flows is the higher of the home or host country rate. This means, for example, that projects should be evaluated as if the maximum permissible amount of dividends were repatriated each year. The fact that there may be substantial tax savings from reinvesting locally, instead of repatriating, is ignored at this initial stage of the investment analysis. The recognition of excess foreign tax credits and alternative, lower-cost remittance channels also should be deferred. Finally, in order to avoid understating the parent's tax liability (by understating remitted cash flow), all funds expected to be transferred to the parent—in the form of management fees, royalties, and licensing fees—are included in this initial stage of the analysis. The reason is simple: If the investment is acceptable under conservative assumptions, it will be acceptable under a more liberal set of circumstances, and there is no need to calculate all the additional tax savings possible. These tax savings can be determined and added back if the initial net present value is negative.

To illustrate the calculation of the incremental tax owed on foreign-source earning, suppose after-tax earnings of $150,000 will be remitted by an affiliate to its U.S. parent in the form of a dividend. Assume the foreign tax rate is 25 percent, the withholding tax on dividends is 4 percent, and excess foreign tax credits are unavailable. The marginal rate of additional taxation is found by adding the withholding tax that must be paid locally, to the U.S. tax owed on the dividend. Withholding tax equals $6,000 ($150,000 × 0.04), while U.S. tax owed equals $12,000. This latter tax is calculated as follows. With a before-tax local income of $200,000 ($200,000 × 0.75 = $150,000), the U.S. tax owed would equal $200,000 × 0.34, or $68,000. The firm then receives foreign tax credits equal to $56,000, for the $50,000 in local tax paid and the

$6,000 dividend withholding tax, leaving a net of $12,000 owed the IRS. This yields a marginal tax rate of 10 percent on remitted profits:

$$\frac{6,000 + 12,000}{150,000} = 0.12.$$

Growth Options and Incremental Project Cash Flows

Any investment which requires an additional infusion of funds for its completion and offers an uncertain payoff can be viewed as a call option. As seen in the case of foreign exchange, a call option gives the holder the *right*, but not the obligation, to buy a security at a fixed, predetermined price (called the *exercise* price) on or before some fixed future date. By way of analogy, the opportunities a firm may have to invest capital so as to increase the profitability of its existing product lines and benefit from expanding into new products or markets may be thought of as *growth options*.[3] Similarly, a firm's ability to capitalize on its managerial talent, experience in a particular product line, its brand name, technology, or its other resources may provide valuable but uncertain future prospects.

Growth options are of great importance to multinational firms.[4] Consider the value of a multinational company's production and market positions in a foreign country at the end of its planning horizon. The MNC may increase or decrease its plant's output, depending on current market conditions, expectations of future demand, and relative cost changes such as those due to currency movements. The plant can be expanded or shut down, then reopened when production and market conditions are more favorable, or abandoned permanently. Each decision is an option from the viewpoint of the firm. The value of these options, in turn, affects the value of the investment in the foreign plant.

Moreover, by producing locally, the MNC will have an enhanced market position in the local market that may enable it to expand its product offerings at a later date. The ability to exploit this market position depends on the results of the firm's research and development efforts and the shifting pattern of demand for its products.

Valuing investments that embody discretionary follow-up projects requires an expanded net present value rule that considers the attendant options. More specifically, the value of an option to undertake a follow-up project equals the expected project NPV, using the conventional discounted cash flow analysis plus the value of the discretion associated with undertaking the project. This is shown in Figure 4–1. The latter element of value (the discretion to invest or not invest in a project) depends on:

1. *The length of time the project can be deferred.* The ability to defer a project gives the firm more time to examine the course of future events and to avoid costly errors if unfavorable developments occur. A longer time interval also raises the odds that a positive turn of events will dramatically boost the project's profitability and turn even a negative NPV project into a positive one.

2. *The risk of the project.* Surprisingly, the riskier the investment the more valuable is an option on it. The reason is the asymmetry between gains and losses. A large gain is possible if the project's NPV becomes highly positive, whereas losses are limited by the option not to exercise when the project NPV is negative. The riskier the project, the greater the odds of a large gain without a corresponding increase in the size of the potential loss. Thus, growth options are likely to be especially valuable for MNCs because of the large potential variation in costs and the competitive environment.

3. *The level of interest rates.* Although a high discount rate lowers the present value of a project's future cash flows, it also reduces the present value of the cash outlay needed to exercise an option. The net effect is that high interest rates generally raise the value of projects that contain growth options.

4. *The proprietary nature of the option.* An exclusively owned option is clearly more valuable than one that is shared with others. Shared options, such as the chance to enter a new market or to invest in a new production process, are less valuable, because competitors can replicate the investments and drive down returns. For the multinational firm, though, most growth options arise out of its intangible assets. These assets, which take the form of skills, knowledge, brand names, and the like, are difficult to replicate and so are likely to be more valuable.

Figure 4–1. Valuing a Growth Option to Undertake a Follow-Up Project

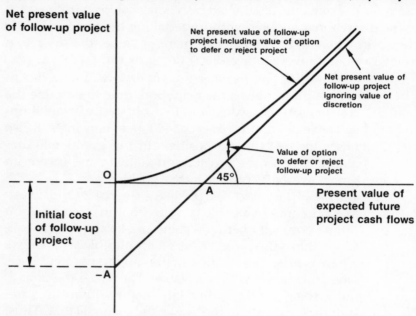

Source: Adapted from W. Carl Kester, "An Options Approach to Corporate Finance," in Edward I. Altman, ed., *Handbook of Corporate Finance,* 5th edition (New York: John Wiley, 1986) 5–27.

Political and Economic Risk Analysis

All else being equal, firms prefer to invest in countries with stable currencies, healthy economies, and minimal political risks. But all else usually is not equal, so firms must devote resources to evaluating the consequences of various political and economic risks for the viability of potential investments.

The three main methods for incorporating the additional political and economic risks, such as the risks of currency fluctuations and expropriation, into foreign investment analyses are:

1. Shortening the minimum payback period.
2. Raising the investment's required rate of return.
3. Adjusting cash flows to reflect the specific impact of a given risk.

Adjust the Discount Rate or Payback Period

The additional risks confronted abroad usually are described in general terms, instead of being related to their impact on specific investments. This rather vague view of risk probably explains the popularity of two questionable approaches to account for the added political and economic risks of overseas operations. One approach is to use a higher discount rate for foreign operations, the other to require a shorter payback period. For instance, if currency controls are anticipated, a normal required return of 15 percent might be raised to 20 percent, or a five-year payback period may be shortened to three years.

Neither of these approaches lends itself to careful evaluation of the actual impact of a particular risk on expected investment returns. Thorough risk analysis requires an assessment of the magnitude and timing of such risks, and their implications for the projected cash flows. For example, an expropriation expected five years hence is likely to be much less threatening than one expected next year, even though there is a higher probability associated with the former. Using a uniformly higher discount rate to reflect these quite different expropriation risks only serves to distort the meaning of a project's present value, by penalizing future cash flows (relatively) more heavily than current ones without obviating the necessity for a careful risk evaluation. Furthermore, the choice of a risk premium (or risk premiums, if the discount rate is allowed to vary over time), whether it is 2 or 10 percent, is arbitrary. Instead, adjusting cash flows makes it possible to fully incorporate all available information about the impact of a specific risk on the future returns from an investment.

Adjust Expected Values

The recommended approach is to adjust a project's cash flows to reflect the *specific* impact of a given risk, primarily because there is normally more and better information on the specific impact of a given risk on a project's cash flows than on its required return.[5] Such cash flow adjustments, by assigning probabilities to various economic and political events, will generate an expected value for the project; that is, the value resulting from this adjustment will reflect the expected mean or average outcome of a number of possible effects on cash flow caused by specific international risks.

While this procedure does not assume that shareholders are risk neutral, it does assume that either (1) risks such as expropriation, currency controls, inflation, and exchange rate changes are unsystematic, or (2) the diversification provided by foreign investment may actually *lower* a firm's systematic risk. If the latter is true (and, as will be argued later, there is evidence to support this belief), adjusting only the expected values of future cash flows will yield a lower bound on the value of the investment to the firm.

According to modern capital market theory, adjusting expected cash flows, instead of the discount rate, to reflect incremental risks is justified so long as the systematic risk of a proposed investment remains unchanged. To the extent that these international economic and political risks are unsystematic, there is no theoretical reason to adjust a project's cost of capital to reflect them. The possibility that foreign investments actually may reduce a firm's systematic risk by supplying international diversification means that, if anything, this approach underestimates a project's present value to the parent corporation.

Although the suggestion that cash flows from politically risky areas should be discounted at a rate that ignores those risks is contrary to current practice, the difference is more apparent than real. As Donald Lessard points out, most firms evaluating foreign investments discount most likely (modal) rather than expected (mean) cash flows at a risk-adjusted rate.[6] If an expropriation or currency blockage is anticipated, then the mean value of the probability distribution of future cash flows will be significantly below its mode. From a theoretical standpoint, of course, cash flows should always be adjusted to reflect the change in expected values caused by a particular risk, but only if the risk is systematic should these cash flows be discounted further.

Exchange Rate Changes and Inflation

Projected cash flows can be stated in nominal (current) or real (constant) domestic or foreign currency terms. Ultimately, to ensure comparability among the various cash flows and with home currency outlays today, all cash flows must be expressed in real terms; i.e., units of constant purchasing power. Nominal cash flows can be converted to real cash flows by adjusting either the cash flows or the discount rate. Both methods yield the same results.[7]

In order to assess the effect of exchange rate changes on expected cash flows, it is necessary first to remove the effect of offsetting inflation and exchange rate changes. It is worthwhile, however, to analyze each effect separately, because there is often a lag between a given rate of inflation and the exchange rate change necessary to maintain international equilibrium. The existence of such a lag—which gives rise to a deviation from purchasing power parity—is most likely when government intervention occurs, such as in a fixed rate system or a system of managed floating. Furthermore, local price controls may not allow the normal adjustment of internal prices to take place.

The possibility of relative price changes within a foreign economy can be incorporated easily by altering projected nominal local currency project cash flows. Thus, the present value of future cash flows can be calculated using a two-stage procedure: (1) convert nominal foreign currency cash flows into nominal home currency terms; and (2) discount those nominal cash flows at the nominal domestic required rate of return. This procedure is identical to converting nominal foreign currency cash flows into *real* home currency terms, and then discounting them at the *real* domestic required rate of return.

Political Risk Measurement and Management

In recent years, there has been a significant increase in developing and developed countries alike in the types and magnitudes of political risks that multinational companies have historically faced. Currency controls, expropriation, changes in tax laws, requirements for additional local production or expensive pollution control equipment are just some of the more visible forms of political risk. The common denominator of such risks, however, is not hard to identify: government intervention into the workings of the economy that affects, for good or ill, the value of the firm. While the consequences are usually adverse, changes in the political environment can provide opportunities. The imposition of quotas on autos from Japan, for example, was undoubtedly beneficial to U.S. automobile manufacturers.

Measuring Political Risk

A number of commercial and academic political risk forecasting models are available today. These models typically supply country indices that attempt to quantify the level of political risk in each nation. Most of these indices rely on some measure(s) of the stability of the local political regime. Such measures may include the frequency of changes of government, the level of violence in the country (for example, violent deaths per 100,000 population), number of armed insurrections, conflicts with other states, and so on. The basic function of these stability indicators is to determine how long the current regime will be in power and whether that regime also will be willing and able to enforce its foreign investment guarantees.

Other popular indicators of political risk include various economic factors such as inflation, balance of payments deficits or surpluses, and the level and growth rate of per capita GNP. The intention behind these measures is to determine whether the economy is in good shape or requires a quick fix such as expropriation, to increase government revenues, or currency inconvertibility, to improve the balance of payments.

One can make a strong case that a good indicator of the degree of political risk is the seriousness of capital flight. *Capital flight* refers to the export of savings by a nation's citizens because of fears about the safety of their financial capital. The risk that most concerns these people is the loss of their capital and savings to expropriation, taxation, or inflation, some or all of which they perceive as possible in their own countries.

Common sense dictates that if a nation's own citizens do not trust the government, then investment there is unsafe. After all, residents presumably have a better feel for conditions and governmental intentions than do outsiders. Thus, when analyzing investment or lending opportunities, multinational firms and international banks must bear in mind the apparent unwillingness of the nation's citizens to invest and lend in their own country.

Despite the increased sophistication of these models, there is little evidence of their ability to successfully forecast political risk. For one thing, political instability by itself does not necessarily contribute to political risk. Changes of government in Latin

America, for example, are quite frequent; yet most multinationals there continue to go about their business undisturbed.

The most important weakness of these indices, however, lies in their assumption that each firm in a country is facing the same degree of political risk. This is manifestly untrue, as is indicated by the empirical evidence on the post–World War II experiences of American and British MNCs. The data clearly show that except in those countries that went Communist, companies differ in their susceptibilities to political risk, depending on their industry, size, composition of ownership, level of technology and degree of vertical integration with other affiliates.[8] For example, expropriation or creeping expropriation is more likely to occur in the extractive, utility, and financial service sectors of an economy than in the manufacturing sector.[9] Also, the expected effect of currency controls probably will not be the same over the life of an investment. It is only when a project is throwing off excess cash that restrictions on profit repatriation generally become a problem.

Because political risk has a different meaning for, and impact on, each firm, it is doubtful that any index of generalized political risk will be of much value to a company selected at random. The specific operating and financial characteristics of a company will largely determine its susceptibility to political risk and, hence, the effects of that risk on the present value of its foreign investment. Rarely do governments, even revolutionary ones, expropriate foreign investments indiscriminately. In general, the greater the perceived benefits to the host economy and the more expensive its replacement by a purely local operation, the smaller the degree of risk to the MNC. The implication is that governments select their expropriation targets according to nonpolitical criteria. Moreover, this degree of selectivity suggests that companies can take actions to control their exposure to political risk.

The selectivity of government targets for expropriation can be explained by viewing the decision to expropriate as being equivalent to the exercise of a call option. Arvind Mahajan points out that when a multinational firm invests in a country it is in effect writing a call option to the host government on its property.[10] The host government will exercise this option—by expropriating the MNC's property—only if the gains exceed the exercise price. The exercise price equals the amount of compensation paid plus the other opportunity costs associated with the expropriation, such as lost export markets and management skills. The option analogy is useful in assessing the effects of various corporate policies for managing political risk. Specifically, the higher the exercise price, the less likely the government will be to expropriate.

Managing Political Risk

Having assessed the political environment of a country, a firm must then decide whether to invest, and if so, how to structure its investment to minimize political risk. Again, the important point to keep in mind is that political risk is not independent of the firm's activities; the configuration of the firm's investments largely will determine their susceptibility to changing government policies. The intent of these policies is to closely link the value of the foreign project to the multinational firm's continued control of the project. By increasing its exercise price, these actions reduce the value of the host government's call option. For example, an MNC can reduce the risk of expropriation by keeping the project dependent on affiliated companies for markets, supplies, transportation, and technology.[11] Another defensive ploy is to offer local investors or government agencies a stake in the venture's success. Similarly, a firm can reduce the impact of currency controls by investing in the form of debt rather than equity (because governments are more hesitant to restrict loan repayments than dividends), borrowing locally, and setting high transfer prices on goods sold to the project while buying goods produced by the project at lower prices where legally possible.[12] Obviously, it is important to incorporate these methods into a capital budgeting and planning procedure that is completed *before* the initial commitment of funds.

One other point: The automatic inclusion of depreciation in computing cash flows from domestic operations is questionable when evaluating a foreign project. Dividend payments in excess of reported profits will decapitalize the enterprise, thereby inviting closer host government scrutiny. Using depreciation cash flows to service parent company debt, however, generally is more acceptable. Moreover, as discussed previously, loan repayments to the parent are received tax free, whereas dividend income is ordinarily taxed. Thus, while parent company funds—whether called debt or equity—require the same return, the cash flow from foreign projects very well could be affected by the form of the investment.

Cash Flow Adjustments for Political Risk

To make the greatest possible use of available information, political risks should be incorporated into foreign investment analysis by adjusting the expected cash flows of a project, not its required rate of return. To demonstrate the application of the proposed cash flow adjustment method, consider the extreme form of political risk—expropriation. The aim of this exercise is to illustrate how an investment analyst could quantify the effect of an expropriation (or any other form of political risk) on the present value of a contemplated foreign investment.

Assume that, in the absence of expropriation, the expected cash flow of a given project over a specified period is $1 million. Assume also that if expropriation occurs during that period, the expected cash flow is zero.[13] If we can assign a probability of expropriation of 0.25, the expected cash flow during that period would be $750,000 (0.75 × $1,000,000 + 0.25 × 0).

Calculating the probability of expropriation with any level of confidence is, of course, impossible. In cases of extreme uncertainty about the timing of a possible expropriation, an alternative to assigning probabilities is to use a form of break-even analysis. Suppose, for instance, that management is reasonably certain that expropriation will occur either in the third year of the project, or not at all. If no expropriation occurs, the project's net present value (NPV) is estimated to be $3 million. If an expropriation does occur, however, the expected NPV is −$2 million. In this case, the expected NPV (in millions) equals $-2p + 3(1 - p)$, where p is the unknown probability of expropriation. The value of p at which the project breaks even can be found by solving for p^* where $-2p^* + 3(1 - p^*) = 0$, or $p^* = 0.6$. Thus, if the probability of expropriation is less than 0.6, the project will have a positive expected net present value. This probability break-even analysis is often more easily applied because it is normally easier, and certainly requires less information, to ascertain whether p is less or greater than .6, than to decide on the absolute level of p.

The Cost of Capital for Foreign Investments

A central question that must be addressed by the multinational corporation is whether the required rate of return on foreign projects should be higher, lower, or the same as that for comparable domestic projects. Although many firms believe that the correct answer is "higher" because of the added political and economic risks involved in investing overseas, this is not necessarily the case.

The cost of capital for a given investment is the minimum risk-adjusted return required by shareholders of the firm undertaking that investment. As such, it is the basic measure of financial performance. Unless the investment generates sufficient funds to compensate the suppliers of capital adequately, the firm's value will suffer. This return requirement is met only if the net present value of project cash flows, discounted at the project's cost of capital, is positive.

The development of appropriate cost of capital measures for MNCs is tied to how those measures will be used. When used as discount rates to aid in the global resource allocation process, they should reflect the value to firms of engaging in specific activities. Thus, the emphasis here is on the cost of capital for specific foreign projects rather than for the firm as a whole. As pointed out earlier, unless the financial structures and commercial risks are similar for all projects considered, the indiscriminate use of an overall cost of capital for project evaluation is inappropriate. Different discount rates should be used to value prospective investments that are expected to change the risk complexion of the firm.

The approach taken here to determine the project-specific required return on equity is based on modern capital market theory. According to this theory, an equilibrium relationship exists between an asset's required return and its associated risk. This relationship can be represented by the *capital asset pricing model* (CAPM). According to the CAPM, intelligent risk-averse shareholders will seek to diversify their risks and, as a result, the only risk that will be rewarded with a risk premium is systematic or nondiversifiable risk. Systematic risk, as measured by beta, is the sensitivity of an investment's value to changes in general economic conditions. Statistically, the beta coefficient is based on the covariance of the investment's returns with broad, marketwide average returns.[14]

Discount Rates for Foreign Projects

The importance of the CAPM for the international firm is that the relevant component of risk in pricing a firm's stock is its systematic risk; in other words, that portion of return variability that cannot be eliminated through diversification. Evidence suggests that most of the economic and political risk faced by MNCs is unsystematic risk, that therefore can be eliminated through diversification on the level of the individual investor. While these risks may be quite large, they should not affect the discount rate to be used in valuing foreign projects.

On the other hand, much of the systematic or general market risk affecting a company, at least as measured using a domestic stock index such as the Standard and Poor's 500 or the New York Stock Exchange index, is related to the cyclical nature of the national economy in which the company is domiciled. Consequently, the returns on a project located in a foreign country whose economy is not perfectly synchronous with the home country's economy should be less highly correlated with domestic market returns than the returns on a comparable domestic project. If this is the case, then the systematic risk of a foreign project actually could well be lower than the systematic risk of its domestic counterpart.

Indirect evidence on the value of corporate international diversification is provided by examining the effects of international portfolio diversification. Donald Lessard[15] and Bruno Solnik,[16] among others, have presented evidence that national factors have more impact on security returns than does any common world factor. In addition, as Table 4-1 shows, returns from the different national equity markets have relatively low correlations with each other.

These results suggest that international diversification significantly reduces the risk of portfolio returns. In fact, as can be seen in Figure 4-1, the variance of an internationally diversified portfolio appears to be as little as 33 percent of the variance of individual securities (as compared to 50 percent for a diversified portfolio of U.S. securities alone). In other words, the risk of an

Table 4–1. How Foreign Markets Correlate With the U.S. Market (1974–83)[a]

Country	Correlation with U.S. Market	Standard Deviation of Returns (percent)	Market Risk (beta) from U.S. Perspective
United States	1.00	18.2	1.00
Canada	0.60	21.9	0.72
United Kingdom	0.33	34.4	0.62
France	0.25	28.8	0.40
West Germany	0.31	19.4	0.33
Switzerland	0.46	23.5	0.59
Italy	0.19	31.5	0.33
Netherlands	0.60	22.6	0.75
Belgium	0.36	22.0	0.44
Austria	0.21	15.0	0.17
Spain	0.06	20.9	0.07
Sweden	0.30	21.7	0.36
Norway	0.25	35.5	0.49
Japan	0.38	20.5	0.43
Hong Kong	0.34	45.5	0.85
Singapore	0.39	41.1	0.88
Australia	0.43	29.3	0.69
World Index[b]	0.91	17.1	0.86

[a]Based on data appearing in *Capital International Perspective*.

[b]Capital International's World Index has a combined market value of $2.1 trillion, covers nineteen countries including the United States, and includes about 1,600 of the largest companies worldwide.

internationally diversified portfolio is about one-third less than the risk of domestically-diversified portfolio.

Paradoxically, it is the less developed countries (LDCs), where political risks are greatest, that are likely to provide the greatest diversification benefits. This is because the economies of LDCs are less closely tied to the United States, or to any other western economy. By contrast, the correlation among the economic cycles of developed countries is considerably stronger, so the diversification benefits from investing in industrialized countries, from the standpoint of an American or western European MNC, are proportionately less.

Figure 4-2. The Potential Gains from International Diversification

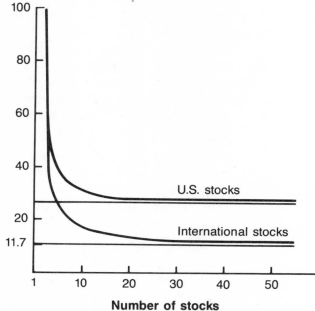

Source: Bruno Solnik, "Why Not Diversify Internationally Rather Than Domestically?" *Financial Analysts Journal* (July–August 1974) 51. Reprinted by permission of the publisher.

It should be noted, however, that the systematic risk of projects even in relatively isolated LDCs is unlikely to be far below the average for all projects, because these countries are still tied into the world economy. The important point about projects in LDCs, then, is that their ratio of systematic to total risk generally is quite low; their systematic risk, while perhaps slightly lower, is probably not significantly less than that of similar projects located in industrialized countries.

Even if a nation's economy is not closely linked to the world economy, the systematic risk of a project located in that country still might be rather large. For example, a foreign copper mining venture probably will face systematic risk very similar to that faced by an identical extractive project in the United States, whether the foreign project is located in Canada, Chile, or Zaire. The reason is that the major element of systematic risk in any extractive project is related to variations in the price of the mineral being extracted, which is set in a world market. The world market price is in turn a function of worldwide demand, which itself is systematically related to the state of the world economy. By contrast, a market-oriented project in an LDC, whose risk depends largely on the evolution of the domestic market in that country, is likely to have a systematic risk that is small both in relative and absolute terms.

An example of the latter would be an automobile plant in Brazil whose profitability is closely linked to the state of the Brazilian economy. The systematic risk of the project, therefore, is largely a function of the correlation between the Brazilian economy and the U.S. economy. While positive, this correlation is likely to be substantially less than one.

Thus, corporate international diversification should prove beneficial to shareholders. But if international portfolio diversification can be accomplished as easily and as cheaply by individual investors, then although required rates of return on MNC securities would be lower to reflect the reduced covariability of MNC returns caused by international diversification, the discount rate would not be reduced further to reflect investors' willingness to pay a premium for the indirect diversification provided by the shares of MNCs. In fact, though, American investors actually undertake very little foreign portfolio investment.

The limited amount of investment in foreign securities normally is explained by the various legal, informational, and economic barriers that serve to segment national capital markets, deterring investors seeking to invest abroad.[17] These barriers include currency controls, specific tax regulations, exchange risk, relatively less efficient and less developed capital markets abroad, and the lack of readily accessible and comparable information on potential foreign security acquisitions. The lack of widespread international portfolio diversification has an important implication for estimating the beta coefficient.

Estimating Project Betas

A major issue when selecting a discount rate for foreign investments is the relevant market portfolio for estimating a project's beta coefficient. Is the relevant base portfolio against which covariances are measured the domestic portfolio of the investor, or the world market portfolio? Selecting the appropriate portfolio matters, because a risk that is systematic in the context of the home country market portfolio may well be diversifiable in the context of the world portfolio. If this is the case, using the domestic market portfolio to calculate beta will result in a higher required return—and a less desirable project—than if beta were calculated using the world market portfolio.

The appropriate market portfolio to use in measuring beta depends on one's view of world capital markets. More precisely, it depends on whether or not capital markets are globally integrated. If they are, then the world portfolio is the correct choice; if they are not, the correct choice is the domestic portfolio. The test of capital market integration does not depend on the correlation, or lack thereof, among returns on assets located in different countries, but rather on whether these assets are priced in a common context; that is, world capital markets are integrated to the extent that security prices offer all investors worldwide the same trade-off between systematic risk and real expected return. In a perfectly integrated market, the risk premium expected by investors for holding a particular stock would reflect that stock's risk relative only to a globally diversified portfolio.

The truth probably lies somewhere in between. Capital markets are now integrated to a great extent, and they can be expected to become ever more so with time. But because of various government regulations and other market imperfections, that integration is not complete. Unfortunately, it is not currently within our power, if indeed it ever will be, to empirically determine the relevant market portfolio and hence the correct beta to use in project evaluation. (Of course, this problem arises domestically as well as internationally.)

A pragmatic recommendation to American managers is to measure the betas of international projects against the U.S. market portfolio. This recommendation is based on the following two reasons:

1. It ensures comparability of foreign with domestic projects, which are evaluated using betas that are calculated relative to a U.S. market index.
2. The relatively minor amount of international diversification attempted (as yet) by American investors suggests that the relevant portfolio from their standpoint is the U.S. market portfolio.

This reasoning suggests that the required return on a foreign project may well be lower, and is unlikely to be higher, than the required return on a comparable domestic project. Thus, applying the same discount rate to an overseas project as to a similar domestic project probably will yield a conservative estimate of the relative systematic riskiness of the project.

Using the domestic cost of capital to evaluate overseas investments also is likely to understate the benefits that stem from the ability of foreign activities to reduce the firm's total risk. As seen in Chapter 1, reducing total risk can increase a firm's cash flows. By confining itself to its domestic market, a firm would be sensitive to periodic downturns associated with the domestic business cycle and other industry-specific factors. By operating in a number of countries, the MNC can trade off negative swings in some countries against positive ones in others. This is especially valuable for non-American firms, whose local markets are small relative to the efficient scale of operation.

Evidence from the Stock Market
The most careful study to date of the effects of foreign operations on the cost of equity capital is by Ali Fatemi.[18] His study compared the performance of two carefully constructed stock portfolios: a portfolio of eighty-four MNCs, each with at least 25 percent of its annual sales generated from international operations, and a portfolio of fifty-two purely domestic firms. Monthly performance comparisons were made over the five-year period of 1976–80.

Although the validity of the study is limited by (1) the relatively short time period involved; (2) the difficulty in properly matching MNCs with their purely domestic counterparts (most firms do business in more than one industry); and (3) in calculating the volume of foreign sales (consider the transfer pricing problem, for example), its conclusions are nonetheless of interest:

1. The rates of return on the two portfolios are statistically identical; ignoring risk, MNCs and uninational corporations (UNCs) provide shareholders the same returns.
2. Consistent with expectations in this text, the rates of return on the MNC portfolio fluctuate less than those on the UNC portfolio. Thus, corporate international diversification seems to reduce shareholders' total risk and may do the same for the firm's total risk.
3. The beta coefficients of the multinational portfolio are significantly lower and more stable than those of the purely domestic portfolio; this indicates that corporate international diversification reduces the degree of systematic risk, at least if systematic risk is calculated relative to the domestic portfolio. It also was found that the higher the degree of international involvement, the lower the beta.

Foreign Investments and Total Risk Reduction

The diversification effect that comes from operating in a number of countries whose economic cycles are not perfectly in phase also could reduce the variability of MNC earnings, in addition to affecting the rate at which these earnings are capitalized. Several studies indicate that this, in fact, is the case.[19] There appears to be little correlation between the earnings of the various national components of MNCs. To the extent that foreign cash flows are not perfectly correlated with those of domestic investments, the overall risk associated with variations in total corporate returns might be *reduced*, not increased, by foreign investments. Thus, on the level of the firm, the greater riskiness of individual projects overseas could well be offset by beneficial portfolio effects. As discussed in Chapter 1, the reduction in a firm's total risk could increase its expected returns. But as pointed out before, this total risk reduction will not affect a foreign project's cost of capital; that depends only on how project returns correlate with market returns.

Corporate Strategy and Foreign Investment

Multinational firms create value for their shareholders by investing overseas in projects that have positive net present values—returns in excess of those required by shareholders.[20] To continue to earn excess returns on foreign projects, multinationals must be able to transfer abroad their sources of domestic competitive advantage. Thus, the emphasis of this section is on how firms create, preserve, and transfer overseas their competitive strengths.

The focus here on competitive analysis and value creation is at odds with the typical capital budgeting process, in which the search for positive NPV projects is confined to estimating future cash flows and the required rates of return on the various investment opportunities (domestic and foreign) facing the firm. Only rarely is the issue raised as to the origin of projects that yield excess returns. Yet selecting positive net present value projects in this way is equivalent to picking undervalued securities on the basis of fundamental analysis. The latter can be done confidently only if financial market imperfections exist that do not allow asset prices to reflect their equilibrium values. Similarly, the existence of economic rents—excess returns that lead to positive net present values—results largely from imperfections in real markets. Such imperfections result from monopolistic control over product or factor markets (a market imperfection). In less technical terms, companies can have a distinctive superiority in knowledge of specific markets, reputation for quality control, service, technological expertise, trademarks, or patents—all of which exist in the real as distinguished from the financial sector of the business.

The imperfections that currently characterize world capital markets are not likely to be present for long. But, unlike the financial sector—where prices are continuously and rapidly adjusting to reflect new information, and where all companies can expect to get a fair deal based on their expected risks and returns—imperfections in the real markets may last for some time. Technological edges, production cost efficiencies, superior management capability, brand names, superior distribution capabilities, vertical integration—all these factors can enable companies to earn consistently abnormal returns. In the long run, though, even such differences can be expected to be neutralized by the inevitable forces of competition.

But over the short to intermediate term, the availability of positive NPV projects depends largely on a company's ability to exploit imperfections in real markets. The essential focus of the corporate planner thus should be on identifying, strengthening, and then capitalizing on those comparative advantages that distinguish the company from actual and potential competitors. A thorough understanding of such imperfections, and the company's ability to exploit them, should provide the qualitative basis for determining—prior to any systematic financial analysis—which foreign projects are likely to have positive net present values.

Various studies of the phenomenon of direct foreign investment—the acquisition abroad of physical assets such as plant and equipment—have helped to identify those market imperfections that have allowed, or encouraged, firms to become multinational. Among those market imperfections are government regulations and controls, such as tariffs and restrictions on capital flows, that impose barriers to free trade and private portfolio investment.

Real market imperfections in the areas of firm-specific skills and information, however, are probably the most important single reason for the rise of multinationals. This is the explanation provided by Richard Caves,[21] who sought to understand not only why firms engage in direct foreign investment, but also why they choose that option over licensing or exporting. Caves's work on multinationals, which relies on the theory of industrial organization, points to certain general circumstances under which each approach—exporting, licensing, or local production—will be the preferred alternative for exploiting foreign markets.

According to Caves, multinationals have intangible capital in the form of trademarks, patents, general marketing skills, and other organizational abilities. If this intangible capital can be embodied without much adaptation in the form of products, an MNC generally will choose exporting as the preferred method of market penetration. Where the firm's knowledge takes the form of specific product or process technologies that can be written down and transmitted objectively, licensing may be the means for foreign expansion.

Often, however, this intangible capital takes the form of organizational skills. Among these specialized skills are knowledge about how best to service a market (including new product development and adaptation), quality control, advertising, distribution, after-sales service, and the general ability to read changing market desires and translate them into sellable products. Because it is difficult, if not impossible, to unbundle these services and sell them apart from the firm, this form of market imperfection often leads to corporate attempts to exert control directly through the establishment of foreign affiliates. There also will, of course, be added costs in establishing and administering an operation overseas. Consequently, internalizing the market for an intangible asset by setting up foreign affiliates makes economic sense if and only if the benefits from circumventing market imperfections outweigh the administrative and other costs of central control.

Because local firms have an inherent cost advantage over foreign investors (who must bear, for example, the costs of operating in an unfamiliar environment along with the stigma of being foreign), multinationals can succeed abroad only if their competitive advantages in, say, technology or marketing skills, cannot be purchased or duplicated by local competitors. Eventually, however, all barriers to entry erode, and the multinational firm must find new sources of competitive advantage to defend itself against the inevitable increase in competition both at home and abroad.

The emphasis for a successful MNC, therefore, must be on systematically pursuing policies and investments congruent with worldwide survival and growth. This approach can be reduced to five interrelated propositions.

First, effective corporate planning should be directed toward identifying those investments likely to provide the most profitable returns. As already seen, these are investments that capitalize on and enhance the differential advantage possessed by the firm; that is, an investment strategy should focus explicitly on building competitive advantage. This could involve a strategy geared to building volume where economies of scale are all-important, or broadening the product scope where economies of scope are critical to success. Such a strategy is likely to encompass a sequence of tactical projects, several of which may yield low returns when considered in isolation, but taken together either create valuable future investment opportunities or allow the firm to continue earning excess returns on existing investments. To properly evaluate a sequence of tactical projects designed to achieve competitive advantage, the projects must be analyzed jointly, rather than incrementally.

For example, if the key to competitive advantage is high volume, the initial entry into a market should be assessed on the basis of its ability to create future opportunities to build market share and the associated benefits thereof. Alternatively, market entry overseas may be judged according to its ability to deter a foreign competitor from launching a market share battle, by the company posing a credible retaliatory threat to the competitor's profit base. By reducing the likelihood of a competitive intrusion, foreign market entry may lead to higher future profits in the home market.

In designing and valuing a strategic investment program, one must be careful to consider the ways in which the investments interact. For example, where scale economies exist, investment in large-scale manufacturing facilities may only be justified if the firm has made supporting investments in foreign distribution and brand awareness. Investments in a global distribution system and a global brand franchise, in turn, are often economical only if the firm has a range of products (and facilities to supply them) that can exploit the same distribution system and brand name.

Developing a broad product line usually requires and facilitates (by enhancing economies of scope) investment in critical technologies that cut across products and businesses. Investments in R&D also yield a steady stream of new products that raises the return on the investment in distribution. At the same time, a global distribution capability may be critical in exploiting new technology.

The return to an investment in R&D is largely determined by the size of the market in which the firm can exploit its innovation and the durability of its technological advantage. As the technology imitation lag shortens, a company's ability to fully exploit a technological advantage may depend on its being able to quickly push products embodying that technology through distribution networks in each of the world's critical national markets.

Individually or in pairs, investments in large-scale production facilities, worldwide distribution, a global brand franchise, and new technology are likely to be negative NPV projects. Together, however, they may yield a highly positive NPV by forming a mutually supportive framework for achieving global competitive advantage.

Secondly, the global approach to investment planning requires a systematic evaluation of individual entry strategies in foreign markets, a comparison of the alternatives, and selection of the best method of entry. For example, in the absence of strong brand names or distribution capabilities, but with a labor cost advantage, Japanese television manufacturers entered the U.S. market by selling low-cost, private-label black and white TVs. Many multinationals seem to disregard the fact that a market's sales potential, and thus its profitability, is at least partly a function of the entry strategy.[22]

Third, investment planning requires a continuous audit of the effectiveness of current entry modes. As knowledge about a foreign market increases, for example, or sales potential grows, the optimal market penetration strategy likely will change. In the case of the Japanese television manufacturers, by the late 1960s they had built a large volume base selling private-label TVs. Using this volume base, they invested in new process and product technologies, from which came the advantages of scale and quality. Recognizing the transient nature of a competitive advantage built on labor and scale advantages, Japanese companies, such as Matsushita and Sony, strengthened their competitive position in the U.S. market by investing throughout the 1970s to build strong brand franchises and distribution capabilities. The new product positioning was facilitated by large-scale investments in R&D. By the 1980s, the Japanese competitive advantage in televisions and other consumer electronics had switched from being cost-based to one based on quality, features, and strong brand names and distribution systems.[23]

Fourth, a systematic investment analysis requires the use of appropriate evaluation criteria. Despite the added complexities of overseas investment evaluations (or perhaps because of the difficulties they present), most MNCs still use simple rules of thumb in making international investment decisions. Analytical techniques are used only as a rough screening device, or as a final checkoff before project approval. While simple rules of thumb are easier and cheaper to use, there is a danger of obsolescence and consequent misuse as the fundamental assumptions underlying their applicability change.

The use of the theoretically sound and recommended present value analysis is anything but straightforward. The strategic rationale underlying many investment proposals can be translated into traditional capital budgeting criteria, but it is necessary to look beyond the returns associated with the project itself to determine its true impact on corporate cash flows and riskiness. For example, an investment made to save a market threatened by competition or trade barriers must be judged on the basis of the sales that would be lost otherwise. Export creation and direct investment also often go hand in hand. ICI, the British chemical company, found that its exports to Europe were enhanced by its strong market position there in other product lines—a position due mainly to ICI's local manufacturing facilities. Such cash flow synergies should be reflected in the capital budgeting analysis.

Applying this concept of evaluating an investment on the basis of its global impact will force companies to answer such tough questions as "How much is it worth to protect our reputation for prompt and reliable delivery?" or "What effect will establishing an operation here have on our present and potential competitors, or on our ability to supply competitive products, and what will be the profit impact of this action?" One possible approach is to determine the incremental costs associated with, say, a defensive action such as building multiple plants (as compared with several larger ones) and then using that number as a benchmark against which to judge how large the present value of the associated benefits (e.g., greater bargaining leverage vis-à-vis host governments) must be to justify the investment.

Fifth and most importantly, the firm must estimate the longevity of its particular form of competitive advantage. If it is easily replicated, it will not take long for both local and foreign competitors to apply the same concept, process, or organizational structure to their operations. The resulting competition will erode profits to a point where the MNC can no longer justify its existence in the market. For this reason, the firm's competitive advantage should be monitored constantly and maintained so as to ensure the existence of an effective barrier to others' entry into the market. Should these barriers to entry break down, the firm must be able to react quickly and either reconstruct them or build new ones. Because no barrier to entry can be maintained indefinitely, however, multinational firms—to remain multinational—must invest continually in developing new competitive advantages that are transferable overseas and that are not easily replicable by the competition.

5

Financing Foreign Operations

The growing internationalization of capital markets and the increased sophistication of companies means that the search for capital no longer stops at the water's edge. This is particularly true for multinational corporations. A distinctive feature of the financial strategy of MNCs is the wide range of external sources of funds that they use on an ongoing basis. General Motors packages car loans as securities and sells them in Europe and Japan. British Telecommunications offers stock in London, New York, and Tokyo, while Beneficial Corporation issues Euroyen notes that may not be sold in either the United States or Japan. Swiss Bank Corporation, aided by Italian, Belgian, Canadian, and German banks, as well as other Swiss banks, helps RJR Nabisco sell Swiss franc bonds in Europe and then swap the proceeds back into U.S. dollars.

International Financing and International Financial Markets

A section in Chapter 3 discussed the rich variety of internal financing options available to the MNC. This section explores the MNC's external medium- and long-term financing alternatives. Those external sources include commercial banks, export financing agencies, public (government) financial institutions, development banks, insurance companies, pension plans, private or public bond and equity placements, and lease financing. While many of the sources are internal to the countries in which the MNCs operate, a growing portion of their funds are coming from offshore markets, particularly the Eurocurrency and Eurobond markets.

Trends in Corporate Financing Patterns

Firms have three general sources of funds available: internally generated cash, short-term external funds, and long-term external funds. External finance can come from investors or lenders. Investors give a company money by buying the securities it issues in the financial markets. These securities, which are generally negotiable (tradable), can take the form of debt, or equity, or some combination of the two, such as convertibles.

The main alternative to issuing public debt securities directly in the open market is to obtain a loan from a specialized financial intermediary that issues securities (or deposits) of its own in the market. These alternative debt instruments usually are commercial bank loans—for short-and medium-term credit—or privately placed bonds—for longer-term credit. Unlike publicly issued bonds, privately placed bonds are sold directly only to a limited number of sophisticated investors, usually life insurance companies and pension funds. Moreover, privately placed bonds are generally nonnegotiable and have complex, customized loan agreements (covenants). The restrictions in the covenants range from limits on dividend payments to prohibitions on asset sales and new debt issues. They provide a series of checkpoints that permit the lender to review actions by the borrower that have the potential to impair the lender's position. These agreements have to be regularly renegotiated prior to maturity. As a result, these privately placed bonds are much more like loans than publicly issued and traded securities.

National Financing Patterns

Figure 5–1 shows that companies in different countries have different financial appetites. Companies in Great Britain get an average of 60 to 70 percent of their funds from internal sources, while West German companies get about 40 to 50 percent of their

Figure 5–1. National Corporate Financing Patterns

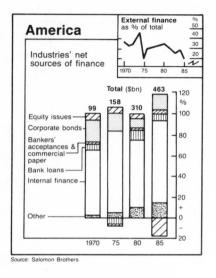

Source: Salomon Brothers

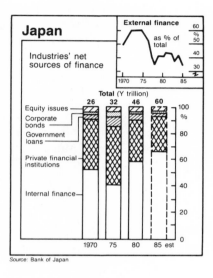

Source: Bank of Japan

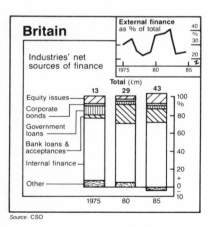

Source: CSO

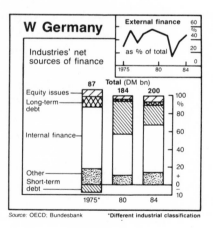

Source: OECD; Bundesbank   *Different industrial classification

Source: Corporate Finance Survey," *The Economist* 7 June 1986

funds from external suppliers.[1] In Japan, where their profitability has been low, companies have relied heavily on external finance. As recently as 1975, Japanese companies got almost 70 percent of their money from outside sources. The shortfall of funds reflected the Japanese strategy of making huge industrial investments and pursuing market share at the expense of profit margins. In 1985, by contrast, almost 70 percent of Japanese corporate funds came from internal sources. The switch from external to internal financing since 1975 is one demonstration of the maturity of Japanese industry.

There has been no comparable transformation in Europe and the United States. Internal finance has consistently supplied the lion's share of financial requirements. The percentage of external finance fluctuates more or less in line with the business cycle; when profits are high, firms are even less reliant on external finance. Moreover, the predominance of internal financing is not accidental. After all, companies could pay out internal cash flow as dividends and issue additional securities to cover their investment needs.

Another empirical regularity about financing behavior relates to the composition of external finance. Regardless of the country studied, debt accounts for the overwhelming share of external funds. By contrast, new stock issues play a relatively small and declining role in financing investment.

Financial Markets Versus Financial Intermediaries

Industry's sources of external finance also differ widely from country to country. West German and Japanese companies rely heavily on bank borrowing, while U.S. and British industry raise much more money directly from financial markets by the sale of securities. In all these countries, however, bank borrowing is on the decline. There is a growing tendency for corporate borrowing to take the form of negotiable securities issued in the public capital markets, rather than in the form of nonmarketable loans provided by financial intermediaries. This process, termed *securitization*, is most pronounced among the Japanese companies. In 1982, 60 percent of their external funds came from borrowing, much of that from banks. Just two years later, that proportion had shrunk to 35 percent.

Securitization largely reflects a reduction in the cost of using financial markets at the same time that the cost of bank borrowing has risen. Until recently, various regulatory restrictions enabled banks to attract low-cost funds from depositors. With financial deregulation, which began in the United States in 1981 and in Japan in 1986, banks must now compete for funds with a wide range of institutions at market rates. In addition, regulatory demands for a stronger capital base have forced U.S. banks to use more equity financing, raising their cost of funds. Inevitably, these changes have pushed up the price of bank loans. Any top flight company can now get money more cheaply by issuing commercial paper than it can from its banks. As a result, banks now have a smaller share of the short-term business credit market.

At the same time, the cost of accessing the public markets is coming down, especially for smaller and less well-known companies. Historically, these companies found it more economical simply to obtain a loan from a bank or to place a private bond issue with a life insurance company. These alternatives proved cheaper because banks and life insurance companies specialize in credit analysis and assume a large amount of borrower's debt. Consequently, they could realize important cost savings in several functions, such as gathering information about the condition of debtor firms, monitoring their actions, and renegotiating loan agreements.

Recent technological improvements in such areas as data manipulation and telecommunications have greatly reduced the costs of obtaining and processing information about the conditions that affect the creditworthiness of potential borrowers. Any analyst now has computerized access, at a relatively low cost, to a wealth of economic and financial information along with programs to store and manipulate this information. Thus investors are now more likely to find it cost effective to lend directly to companies, rather than indirectly through financial intermediaries such as commercial banks. This borrowing often takes the form of low-grade or "junk" bonds.

These same advances in communications and technology, together with financial deregulation abroad, have blurred the distinction between domestic and foreign financial markets. As the necessary electronic technology has been developed and the costs of transactions have plummeted, the world has become one vast interconnected market. Markets for U.S. government securities and certain stocks, foreign exchange trading, interbank borrowing and lending—to cite a few examples—operate continuously and in enormous size around the clock and around the world. Globalization has brought about an unprecedented degree of competition among key financial centers and financial institutions that has further reduced the costs of issuing new securities.

International Financial Markets

International financial markets can develop anywhere, provided that local regulations permit and that the potential users are attracted to the market. Some governments such as the French and Japanese (until recently) actively discourage foreign participation in their local markets, while others such as Spain and Turkey may favor the internationalization of their capital markets but are unable to attract the business.

The most important international financial centers are London and New York. All the other major industrial countries have important domestic financial markets as well, but only some, such as Germany and—recently—Japan, are also important international financial centers. On the other hand, some countries which have relatively unimportant domestic financial markets are important world financial centers. The markets of those countries, which include Switzerland, Luxembourg, Singapore, Hong Kong, the Bahamas, and Bahrain, serve as financial entrepôts—channels through which foreign funds pass. That is, these markets serve as financial intermediaries between nonresident suppliers of funds and nonresident users of funds.

Political stability and minimal government intervention are prerequisites for becoming and remaining an important international financial center, especially an entrepôt center. Governments, however, are usually unwilling to rely completely on the market to perform the functions of gathering and allocating funds. In most countries, the government intervenes either directly, through state-controlled financial institutions, or indirectly, through state-supplied subsidies, to channel funds to certain favored industries (e.g., shipbuilding), or business activities (e.g., exporting).

Foreign Access to Domestic Markets

Foreigners are often hampered in their ability to gain access to domestic capital markets because of government-imposed or suggested restrictions relating to the maturities and amounts of money that they can raise; as well as the government-legislated extra costs such as special taxes—e.g., the U.S. Interest Equalization Tax (IET) that was in effect from 1963 to 1974—that they must bear on those funds which they can raise. Nonetheless, the financial markets of many countries are open wide enough to permit foreigners to borrow or invest.

As a citizen of many nations, the multinational firm has greater leeway in tapping a variety of local money markets than does a purely domestic firm, but the multinational too is often the target of restrictive legislation aimed at reserving local capital for indigenous companies or the local government. The capital that can be raised is frequently limited to local uses through the imposition of exchange controls. As seen previously, however, multinationals are potentially capable of transferring funds, even in the presence of currency controls, by using a variety of financial channels. To the extent, therefore, that local credits substitute for parent- or affiliate-supplied financing, the additional monies are available for removal.

The Foreign Bond Market

The foreign bond market, an important part of the international financial markets, is simply that portion of the domestic bond market that represents issues floated by foreign companies or governments. As such, foreign bonds are subject to local laws and must be denominated in the local currency. At times these issues face additional restrictions as well. For example, foreign bonds floated in Switzerland, Germany, and the Netherlands are subject to a queuing system.

The United States and Switzerland contain the most important foreign bond markets. Major foreign bond markets are also located in Japan, Germany, and the Netherlands. Data on the amounts and currency denominations of foreign bond issues are presented in Table 5-1.

Table 5-1. Foreign Bond Issue: Breakdown by Market of Issue (In millions of U.S. dollars)

Market	1984	Percent	1985	Percent	1986	Percent
Austria	42	0.1	72	0.2	84	0.2
Belgium	164	0.6	282	0.9	345	0.9
Canada	156	0.6	147	0.5		
Finland					49	0.1
France	21	0.1	417	1.3	477	1.2
Germany	2,419	8.6	1,741	5.6		
Ireland			18	0.1		
Italy			257	0.8	210	0.5
Japan	4,873	17.3	6,255	20.0	5,223	13.3
Kuwait						
Luxembourg	202	0.7	400	1.3	816	2.1
Netherlands	1,157	4.1	979	3.1	1,724	4.4
Sweden					43	0.1
Switzerland	13,120	46.7	14,873	47.6	23,213	59.0
United Kingdom	1,649	5.9	873	2.8	394	1.0
United States	4,294	15.3	4,917	15.7	6,782	17.2
Total	28,097	100	31,229	100	39,359	100

Source: Organization for Economic Cooperation and Development, *Financial Market Trends,* various issues.

The Foreign Banking Market

The foreign bank market represents that portion of domestic bank loans supplied to foreigners for use abroad. As in the case of foreign bond issues, governments often restrict the amounts of bank funds destined for foreign purposes. During the 1960s, for example, the U.S. government imposed the "voluntary" Foreign Credit Restraint Program (it later became mandatory), which greatly constrained the ability of U.S. banks to lend money to foreign borrowers and even to U.S. firms for use overseas.

The importance of foreign banks as a funding source is obvious when one examines Table 5-2, which contains the roster of the world's ten largest banks in terms of assets as of August 30, 1986. Note that eight of the ten largest banks, including the top four, are Japanese banks. The only American bank in this ranking is Citicorp, and it is only fifth largest.

Table 5–2. The World's Ten Largest Banking Concerns
Ranked by Assets; Converted into U.S. Dollars as of
August 30, 1986

Bank	Assets in billions of U.S. dollars
1. Dai-Ichi Kangyo Bank	$201.8
2. Fuji Bank	199.3
3. Sumitomo Bank	187.2
4. Mitsubishi Bank	173.7
5. Citicorp	173.6
6. Sanwa Bank	168.7
7. Mitsubishi Trust & Banking	142.3
8. Norinchukin Bank	139.9
9. Banque Nationale de Paris	139.6
10. Industrial Bank of Japan	139.5

Source: "Special Report on Global Finance and Investing," *Wall Street Journal* 29 September 1986, p. 18D.

The Foreign Equity Market

The idea of placing stock in foreign markets has long attracted corporate finance managers. One attraction is the diversification of equity funding risk: A pool of funds from a diversified shareholder base insulates a company from the vagaries of a single national market. For large companies located in small countries, foreign sales may be a necessity.

Selling stock overseas also increases the potential demand for the company's shares by attracting new shareholders. The added demand may enhance valuation. A study by Gordon Alexander, Cheol Eun, and S. Janakiramanan[2] found that foreign companies which listed their shares in the United States experienced a decline in their expected return. This evidence is consistent with the theoretical work of Robert Merton,[3] who shows that a company can lower its cost of equity capital by expanding its investor base. Moreover, for a firm that wants to project an international presence, an international stock offering can spread the firm's name in local markets.

Despite these advantages, the advent of stock issues specifically structured for, and directed toward, foreign markets has occurred only in the past few years. Today a growing number of American and European companies are selling stock issues overseas. For example, three of the fifteen largest equity offerings in the United States in 1984 were made by British companies (British Telecom, $278.9 million; Reuters, $107.2 million; and Cadbury Schweppes, $102 million).

International equity placements generally fall into one of two categories. U.S. companies typically issue *dual syndicate equity offerings* such as the Bear Stearns issue, where the offering is split into two tranches—domestic and overseas—and each tranche is handled by a separate lead manager. In contrast, European companies mostly offer *Euroequity issues*—single tranche syndicated equity offerings placed throughout Europe and handled by one lead manager.

Most major stock exchanges permit sales of foreign issues provided the issue satisfies all the listing requirements of the local market. Some of the major stock markets list large numbers of foreign stocks. For example, Union Carbide, Black and Decker, Caterpillar, and General Motors are among the more than 200 foreign stocks listed on the German stock exchanges. Similarly, over 500 foreign stocks, including ITT, Hoover, and Woolworth, are listed on the British exchanges. More companies are also seeking to be listed on the Tokyo Stock Exchange. The New York Stock Exchange listed 56 foreign stocks as of January 1, 1987, with another 49 traded on the American Stock Exchange.

The Euromarkets

This section describes the functioning of the Eurocurrency and Eurobond markets and shows how each can be used to meet the multinational firm's financing requirements.

The Eurocurrency Market

A *Eurocurrency* is a dollar or other freely convertible currency deposited in a bank outside its country of origin. Thus, dollars on deposit in London become Eurodollars. These deposits can be placed in a foreign bank or in the foreign branch of a domestic U.S. bank. The Eurocurrency market then consists of those banks (Eurobanks) that accept deposits and make loans in foreign currencies.

The most important characteristic of the Eurocurrency market is that loans are made on a floating-rate basis. Interest rates on loans to governments and their agencies, corporations, and non-prime banks are set at a fixed margin above the London interbank offer rate (LIBOR) for the given period and currency chosen. At the end of each period, the interest for the next period is calculated at the same fixed margin over the new LIBOR. For example, if the margin is 0.75 percent and the current LIBOR is 13 percent, then the borrower is charged 13.75 percent for the upcoming period. The period normally chosen is six months, but shorter periods such as one month or three months are possible. However, the administrative inconvenience and cost of *rolling over* a loan every one or three months is an important factor in choosing a six-month rollover period. The LIBOR used, of course, corresponds to the maturity of the rollover period.

The *margin*, or spread between the lending bank's cost of funds and the interest charged the borrower, varies a good deal among borrowers and is based on the borrower's perceived riskiness. Typically, such spreads have ranged from slightly below 0.5 percent to over 3 percent, with the median being somewhere between 1 and 2 percent.

The maturity of a loan can vary from approximately three to ten years. Maturities have tended to lengthen over time, from a norm of about five years originally to eight to ten years these days for prime borrowers. Lenders in this market are almost exclusively banks. In any single loan, there will normally be a number of participating banks that form a syndicate. The bank originating the loan will usually manage the syndicate. This bank, in turn, may invite one or two other banks to comanage the loan.

The manager(s) charge(s) the borrower a once-and-for-all fee or commission of 0.25 to 1 percent of the loan value, depending on the size and type of the loan. Part of this fee is kept by the manager(s), and the rest is divided up among all the participating banks [including the manager(s)] according to the amount of funds each bank supplies.

The capacity of the market seems capable of accommodating the needs of almost any borrower in amounts ranging from $500,000 to $1 billion and more.

The *drawdown* (the period over which the borrower may take down the loan) and the repayment period vary in accordance with the borrower's needs. A commitment fee, usually about 0.5 percent per annum, is paid on the unused balance, and prepayments are permitted, sometimes subject to a penalty fee.

Eurobonds

Eurobonds are similar in many respects to the public debt sold in domestic capital markets. Unlike domestic bond markets, however, the Eurobond market is almost entirely free of official regulation, but instead is self-regulated by the Association of International Bond Dealers. The prefix "Euro" refers to the fact that the bonds are sold outside the countries in whose currencies they are denominated. The Eurobond and Eurocurrency markets are often confused with each other, but there is a fundamental distinction between them. Eurobonds are issued by the final borrowers directly, whereas the Eurocurrency market enables investors to hold short-term claims on banks which then act as intermediaries to transform these deposits into long-term claims on final borrowers. However, banks, in their capacity as underwriters, do play an important role in placing these bonds with the final investors.

Although there are significant conceptual and practical problems in measuring the size of the Eurocurrency market (e.g., should it be measured on the basis of gross or net liabilities?), the Eurobond market, until recently, has been the substantially smaller market. Borrowers in the Eurobond market must be well known and must have impeccable credit ratings; e.g., developed countries, international institutions, and large multinational corporations. Even then the amounts raised in the Eurobond market have, historically, been far less than those in the Eurocurrency market.

As can be seen from Table 5–3, however, the Eurobond market has exhibited phenomenal growth in recent years. From 1981 through 1986, the volume of new Eurobond issues surged sixfold to $187 billion, making the Eurobond market by far the largest capital raising market outside the United States. By contrast, new-issue volume in the U.S. corporate bond market totaled about $180 billion in 1986.

Table 5–3.
Eurobond Issues: Breakdown by Currency of Issue
In millions of U.S. dollars

Currency	1979	Percent	1980	Percent	1981	Percent	1982	Percent	1983	Percent
United States dollar	12,565	67.1	16,427	68.5	26,830	84.9	43,959	85.1	38,406	79.2
Deutsche mark	3,626	19.4	3,607	15.0	1,277	4.0	2,588	5.0	3,776	7.8
Canadian dollar	425	2.3	279	1.2	634	2.0	1,201	2.3	1,039	2.1
Dutch guilder	531	2.8	1,043	4.4	529	1.7	645	1.2	735	1.5
French franc	342	1.8	986	4.1	533	1.7	4	0.0		0.0
Japanese yen	116	0.6	304	1.3	368	1.2	374	0.7	212	0.4
Pound sterling	291	1.6	974	4.1	501	1.6	748	1.4	1,915	3.9
ECUs	253	1.4	65	0.3	309	1.0	1,980	3.8	2,095	4.3
Other	577	3.1	285	1.2	635	2.0	146	0.3	305	0.6
Total	18,726	100	23,970	100	31,616	100	51,645	100	48,483	100

Currency	1984	Percent	1985	Percent	1986	Percent	1987	Percent
United States dollar	65,334	80.2	96,822	70.9	118,096	62.9	56,727	40.4
Deutsche mark	4,324	5.3	9,612	7.0	17,127	9.1	15,518	11.0
Canadian dollar	2,147	2.6	2,912	2.1	5,067	2.7	5,891	4.2
Dutch guilder	689	0.8	649	0.5	973	0.5	1,237	0.9
French franc			1,123	0.8	3,523	1.9	1,899	1.4
Japanese yen	1,190	1.5	6,615	4.8	18,516	9.9	23,116	16.5
Pound sterling	3,965	4.9	6,130	4.5	10,585	5.6	14,997	10.7
ECUs	2,938	3.6	6,903	5.1	7,057	3.8	7,423	5.3
Other	834	1.0	5,777	4.2	6,804	3.6	13,673	9.7
Total	81,420	100	136,543	100	187,747	100	140,481	100

Since 1986, however, the Eurobond market has been in a deep slump. New Eurobond issues tumbled 28 percent in 1987 to $134 billion, the first drop in five years. The dollar-denominated part of the market was hardest hit; its share of new offerings plummeted to less than 42 percent in 1987 from nearly 85 percent in 1982.

Because of its size and relatively low interest rates, virtually every treasurer, from multinational corporations to the U.S. government, still considers the Eurobond market an important source of funding. But its importance is diminishing, at least for U.S. companies. The Eurobond market's share of U.S. corporate debt financings declined in 1986 and again in 1987; after providing almost 25 percent of the money raised by U.S. corporate issuers in 1985, the Eurobond market provided only 16 percent in 1986 and less than 8 percent in 1987.

The slump in Eurobond financing is attributed in part to the dollar's weakness. Although more foreign investors are buying U.S. securities, most of them still turn first to the Euromarket for dollar-denominated bonds. Thus, if foreigners want to diversify out of dollar bonds, the Euromarket gets hit first. This is reflected in the declining share of dollar-denominated Eurobonds. Another possible reason is the substitution of Euronotes, which are not included in the figures, for Eurobonds.

Most importantly, perhaps, with the repeal in 1984 of U.S. withholding tax on interest paid to foreign bondholders and financial market deregulation in the United States and elsewhere, the Eurobond market lost much of the cost advantage that lured borrowers and investors in the first place. By lowering the cost of issuing bonds in the U.S. and dramatically accelerating the issuing process, financial deregulation and repeal of withholding tax improved the competitive position of the U.S. capital market relative to the Eurobond market. Other nations such as Japan, France, and England also embarked on a program of deregulating their financial markets.

The growing presence of sophisticated investors willing to arbitrage between the domestic dollar and Eurodollar bond markets, in part because the United States no longer imposes withholding taxes on foreign investors, has eliminated much of the interest disparity that existed between Eurobonds and domestic bonds. Despite the closer alignment of the two markets, though, the Eurobond issuer may, at any given time, take advantage of Eurobond "windows" when a combination of domestic regulations, tax laws, and expectations of international investors enable the issuer to achieve a lower all-in financing cost—often involving currency and interest swaps—than is available in domestic markets. In addition to the possibility of reduced borrowing costs, the Eurobond issuer may diversify its investor base and funding sources by having access to the international Eurocapital markets of Western Europe, North America, and the Far East.

In 1984, for the first time, the volume of Eurodollar floating-rate note (FRN) issues exceeded the supply of conventional fixed-rate Eurodollar bonds. The boom in FRN financings also spawned a related market in Eurodollar short-term notes, maturing in one year or less, for countries and companies. It is projected that this market will continue to grow at the expense of banks. This is part of the process of securitization discussed earlier in this chapter.

Eurobond issues are arranged through an underwriting group, often with 100 or more underwriting banks involved for an issue as small as $25 million. A growing volume of Eurobonds is being placed privately, for several very attractive reasons:

1. *Simplicity*. No prospectus needs to be printed, and the offering memorandum is brief.
2. *Speed*. The total time involved in bringing an issue to market and selling it can be measured in weeks, not months.
3. *Privacy*. There are no lengthy disclosure statements necessary.
4. *Lower cost*. Since the underwriting group also sells the issue, there is no need to pay financial intermediaries. Legal costs are also lower.

Due to the lower overall issuing costs involved, borrowers are often willing to provide higher yields, giving investors an incentive to tie up their funds for longer periods of time than in the public Eurobond market.

Historically, about 75 percent of Eurobonds have been dollar denominated. During the late 1970s, however, when the dollar was in a downward spiral, other currencies, particularly the deutsche mark, became more important in the Eurobond market. Deutsche mark-denominated new Eurobond issues reached a peak of 17 percent in 1980. The sharp increase in the share of dollar-denominated Eurobonds in the period up to mid-1985 largely reflects the surging value of the dollar. The more recent drop in the dollar's value has again led to a rise in non-dollar issues, particularly yen and deutsche mark issues. The absence of Swiss franc Eurobonds is due to the Swiss Central Bank's ban on using the Swiss franc for Eurobond issues.

As an alternative to issuing dollar, deutsche mark, or other single currency-denominated Eurobonds, several borrowers in recent years have offered bonds whose value is a weighted average or "basket" of several currencies. The most successful of these currency "cocktails" is the European Currency Unit (ECU). Although they have failed to capture a significant share of the Eurobond market, ECU issues have become a growing segment of the market.

ECU bonds offer advantages to both investors and borrowers, including the following:

1. **Access to markets that might not otherwise be available.** The markets for some individual European currencies are not very liquid and certain European capital markets such as the Belgian franc, French franc, Italian lira, and Danish krone bond markets, are difficult to tap directly for funds because of remaining capital controls. Using the ECU therefore lowers transaction costs, enables indirect access to currencies otherwise unavailable, and allows wider market diversification.

2. **Diversification of currency risk,** especially for investors and borrowers within the European Monetary System. The effect of weakening currencies will—to some degree— be offset by strengthening currencies within the basket. Although the currency percentage contained in an ECU bond is probably suboptimal in terms of its risk-return trade-off, investors and borrowers dealing in ECUs may face lower transaction costs than if they were to tailor their own currency baskets.

3. **A hedge against the dollar.** Because the ECU basket excludes the dollar completely, the value of the ECU—in terms of any of its component currencies—is generally unaffected by changes in the value of the dollar.

Secondary Market

Historically, there has been a lack of depth in the Eurobond secondary market (the market where investors trade securities that have already been bought). However, the growing number of institutions carrying large portfolios of Eurobonds for trading purposes has increased the depth and sophistication of this market, making it second only to the U.S. domestic bond market in liquidity (where liquidity refers to the ease of trading securities at close to their quoted price). Until recently, the liquidity of Eurobonds has not mattered because investors were usually willing to purchase and lock such issues away. But because of heightened volatility in bond and currency markets, investors increasingly want assurance that they can sell Eurobonds before maturity at bid-ask spreads (the difference between the buy and the sell rate, which is a major determinant of liquidity) comparable to those in other capital markets.

One problem is that there is no central trading floor where dealers post prices. Hence, buyers sometimes have difficulty getting price quotes on Eurobonds. However, many commercial banks, investment banks, and securities trading firms act as market makers in a wide range of issues, quoting two-way prices (buy and sell), and being prepared to deal at those prices. Another factor adding liquidity to the market is the presence of bond brokers. They act as middlemen, taking no positions themselves but transacting orders when a counterparty is found to match a buy or sell instruction. Brokers deal only with market makers and never with the ultimate investor.

Despite the high degree of liquidity in the market overall, there are specific issues, especially those with longer maturities, that have liquidity problems. To address some of the concerns of Eurobond buyers about the liquidity of their issues, the International Primary Market Association asked members that syndicate fixed-rate Eurodollar bonds to pledge that they will make markets in the bonds they sell for as long as one year after their issuance.

Eurobonds Versus Eurocurrency Loans

Both Eurocurrency and Eurobond financing have their advantages and disadvantages. Although many of these factors are reflected in the relative borrowing costs, not all factors are so reflected. For a given firm, therefore, and for a specific set of circumstances, one method of financing may be preferred to the other. The differences are categorized in five ways.

1. *Cost of borrowing.* Eurobonds are issued in both fixed- and floating-rate forms. Fixed-rate bonds are an attractive exposure management tool since known long-term currency inflows can be offset with known long-term outflows in the same currency. By contrast, the interest rate on a Eurocurrency loan is variable, making Eurocurrency loans better hedges for noncontractual currency exposures. The variable interest rate benefits borrowers when rates decline, but hurts them when rates rise. Arbitrage between

Eurobonds and Eurocurrencies, however, should not provide a certain cost advantage to one or the other form of borrowing.

2. *Maturity.* While the period of borrowing in the Eurocurrency market has tended to lengthen over time, Eurobonds still have longer maturities.

3. *Size of issue.* Until recently, the amount of loanable funds available at any one time has been much greater in the interbank market than in the bond market. In 1983, for the first time, the volume of Eurobond offerings exceeded voluntary global bank lending (those loans not forced by debt reschedulings). In many instances, borrowers have discovered that the Eurobond market can easily accommodate financings of a size and at a price not previously thought possible. When Digital Equipment, Texas Instruments, International Paper, and Illinois Power brought out $475 million of Eurodollar bonds over two days in February 1984, they saved as much as 0.45 percent on the cost of issuing debt in the United States. This translates into millions of dollars of interest savings. Moreover, although in the past the flotation costs of a Eurocurrency loan have been much lower than on a Eurobond (about 0.5 percent of the total loan amount versus about 2.25 percent of the face value of a Eurobond issue), competition has worked to lower Eurobond flotation costs.

4. *Flexibility.* In the case of a Eurobond issue, the funds must be drawn down in one sum on a fixed date and repaid according to a fixed schedule unless the borrower pays an often substantial prepayment penalty. By contrast, the drawdown in a floating-rate loan can be staggered to suit the borrower's needs, with a fee of about 0.5 percent per annum paid on the unused portion (normally much cheaper than drawing down and redepositing) and can be prepaid in whole or in part at any time, often without penalty. Moreover, a Eurocurrency loan with a multicurrency clause enables the borrower to switch currencies on any rollover date, whereas switching the denomination of a Eurobond from Currency A to Currency B would require a costly, combined refunding and reissuing operation. A much cheaper and comparable alternative, however, would be to sell forward for Currency B an amount

of Currency A equal to the value of the Eurobond issue still outstanding. There is a rapidly growing market in such currency swaps that enable the proceeds from bonds issued in one currency to be converted into money in another currency.

5. *Speed*. Internationally known borrowers can raise funds in the Eurocurrency market very quickly, often within two to three weeks of first request. A Eurobond financing generally takes more time to put together, although here again the difference is becoming less significant.

Note Issuance Facilities

Eurobanks have responded to the competition from the Eurobond market by creating a new instrument—the note issuance facility (NIF). The NIF, which is a low-cost substitute for syndicated credits, allows borrowers to issue their own short-term notes, which are then placed or distributed by the financial institutions providing the NIF. NIFs, sometimes also called short-term note issuance facilities or SNIFs, have some features of the U.S. commercial paper market and some features of U.S. commercial lines of credit. Like commercial paper, notes under NIFs are unsecured short-term debt generally issued by large corporations with excellent credit ratings. Indeed, NIFs are sometimes referred to as Eurocommercial paper. Like loan commitments in the United States, NIFs generally include multiple pricing components for various contract features, including a market-based interest rate and one or more fees known as participation, facility, and underwriting fees. Participation fees are paid when the contract is formalized and are generally about 10 basis points (100 basis points equals 1 percent) multiplied by the facility size. Other fees are paid annually, and are sometimes based on the full size of the facility, sometimes on the unused portions thereof.

Many NIFs include underwriting services as part of the arrangements. When they are included, the arrangement generally takes the form of a revolving underwriting facility (RUF). The RUF gives borrowers long-term continuous access to short-term money underwritten by banks at a fixed margin.

NIFs are more flexible than floating-rate notes and usually cheaper than syndicated loans. Banks eager to beef up their earnings without fattening their loan portfolios (which would then require them to add expensive equity capital) made NIFs an important new segment of the Euromarket. By early 1986, more than $75 billion of facilities had been arranged. As in the case of floating-rate notes, the popularity of NIFs benefits from the market's current preference for lending to high-grade borrowers through securities rather than bank loans. Figure 5–2 shows the rapid growth of NIFs, clearly at the expense of the Eurocurrency loan market (represented by syndicated bank loans).

The basic facility works in the following manner (although alternate methods exist in abundance in the marketplace): A syndicate of banks underwrites an amount—usually about $50 to $200 million—for a specified period, typically for five to seven years. A LIBOR-based underwriting margin is set, determined by the credit rating of the borrower, the size of the issue, and market conditions. When the borrower decides to draw on the facility, he/she can choose to issue promissory notes, called Euronotes, with one-, three-, six-, or twelve-month maturities. A tender panel of banks is then established, whose members submit competitive bids. Any bids above the agreed underwriting margin are not accepted. These are automatically purchased by the underwriters at the agreed-upon margin over LIBOR.

In effect, NIFs are put options, giving borrowers the right to sell their paper to the bank syndicate at a price that yields the prearranged spread over LIBOR. Borrowers will exercise this right only if they cannot place their notes at a better rate elsewhere (this is most likely to happen if their creditworthiness deteriorates). The primary risk to the banks, therefore, is that they might someday have to make good on their pledge to buy paper at a spread that is too low for the credit risks involved. Although Euronote issuers generally are firms with sound credit standing, a NIF may oblige the banks to keep rolling the notes over for five to ten years—time enough for even the best credit risk to turn into a nightmare.

Most Euronotes are denominated in U.S. dollars and are issued with high face values (often $500,000 or more). They are

Figure 5–2. International Financial Market Activity

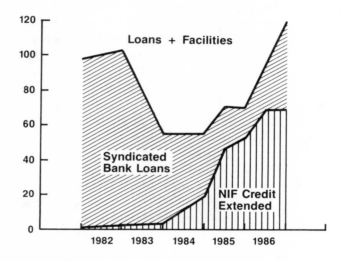

$ Billions

Source: Steven E. Plaut, "NIF, SNIF, RUF, Gesundheit," *FRBSF Weekly Letter,* Federal Reserve Bank of San Francisco, October 9, 1987, p. 3.

intended for professional or institutional investors, rather than private individuals. The average size of facilities has grown from under $200 million in 1982 to over $500 million by 1986. However, the proportion of facilities actually drawn remains quite low, with no more than 10 to 20 percent of Euronotes outstanding under the NIFs at any one time.

Note Issuance Facilities Versus Eurobonds

In addition to their lower direct costs, NIFs offer several other benefits to the issuer relative to floating-rate notes, their most direct competitor:

    1. *Drawdown flexibility.* Note issuers can usually opt to draw down all or part of their total credit whenever their need arises, and can roll over portions at will. This is especially valuable for borrowers with seasonal or cyclical needs.

151

2. *Timing flexibility.* With FRNs, the borrower must live with the prevailing rate for the duration of the period. By contrast, if a Euronote borrower thinks rates are going to fall, the borrower can wait a month or so to issue. However, unless the financial director is better able to forecast interest rates, this is a dubious advantage.

3. *Choice of maturities.* FRN issuers are generally locked into one maturity setting—three months or six months—over the life of the deal. NIFs, on the other hand, give borrowers the choice of issuing notes with different maturities whenever they choose to draw down new debt or roll over old debt.

4. *Secondary market.* The secondary market for Euronotes is relatively undeveloped compared to the market for FRNs. This makes Euronotes less liquid, limiting Euronote investors to those who want to hold them to maturity.

Special Financing Vehicles

This section examines two special financing vehicles that multinational corporations can use to fund their foreign investments. These vehicles include interest rate and currency swaps and bank loan swaps. Each of them presents opportunities to the multinational firm to reduce financing costs and/or risk.

Swaps

The major catalyst for growth in the Eurobond market over the last few years has been the emergence of a technique known as the *swap*, a financial transaction in which two counterparties agree to exchange streams of payments over time. It is now estimated that 70 percent of Eurobond issues are "swap driven." Swaps allow borrowers to raise money in one market and to swap one interest rate structure for another (e.g., from fixed to floating), or to go further and swap principal and interest from one currency to another. These swaps allow the parties to the contract to arbitrage their relative access to different currency markets; a borrower whose paper is much in demand in one currency can obtain a cost saving in another currency sector by raising money in the former and swapping the funds into the latter currency.

It is now the rule rather than the exception that a series of swaps have to be constructed to fulfill the Eurobond issuer's financial objective. For example, a borrower may find that the cheapest way to raise U.S. dollars one day may be via a fixed-rate Australian dollar issue swapped into U.S. dollars floating at LIBOR, and in turn, swapped into fixed-rate U.S. dollars. The next day, however, movements in any one of the markets may mean that the best route to cheaper fixed-rate U.S. dollars is through a floating-rate sterling issue swapped directly into fixed-rate dollars.

The swaps market has become increasingly important to corporate financial managers. They can use swaps to arrange complex, innovative financings that reduce borrowing costs and increase control over interest rate risk and foreign currency exposure. As a result of the deregulation and integration of national capital markets and extreme interest rate and currency volatility, the relatively new swaps market has experienced explosive growth, with a 1986 volume in excess of $350 billion. In fact, estimates indicate that of the $200 billion of international bond issues transacted in 1986, close to 80 percent were swap related.

Swaps have had a major impact on the treasury function, permitting firms to tap new capital markets and to take further advantage of innovative products without an increase in risk. Through the swap, they can trade a perceived risk in one market or currency for a liability in another. The swap has led to a refinement of risk management techniques, which in turn has facilitated corporate involvement in international capital markets.

There are three major types of swaps:

1. *Interest rate swap.* This is an agreement to change debt from floating rate into fixed rate or vice versa. Typically, principal is not exchanged; only the interest is actually paid by each party.
2. *Currency swap.* This is an agreement to transform an obligation in one currency to one in another.
3. *Interest rate/currency swap.* This agreement converts a liability in one currency with a stipulated type of interest payment, into one denominated in another currency, with a different type of interest payment.

The following example illustrates an *interest rate/currency swap,* the most complex of the three.

Kodak's Zero-Coupon Australian Dollar Interest Rate/Currency Swap

In late March Eastman Kodak Company, a AAA-rated firm, indicated to Merrill Lynch that it needed to raise U.S. $400 million.[4] Kodak's preference was to fund through nontraditional structures, obtaining U.S. $200 million for both five and ten years. Kodak stated that it would spend up to two weeks evaluating non-dollar financing opportunities for the five-year tranche, targeting a minimum size of U.S. $75 million and an all-in cost of U.S. Treasuries plus 35 basis points. In contrast, a domestic bond issue by Kodak would have to be priced to yield about U.S. Treasuries plus 50 basis points. At the end of the two-week period, the remaining balance was to be funded with a competitive bid.

After reviewing a number of potential transactions, the Capital Markets group at Merrill Lynch decided that investor interest in non-dollar issues was much stronger in Europe than in the United States, and that Merrill Lynch should focus on a non-dollar Euroissue for Kodak. Merrill Lynch's London Syndicate Desk informed its Capital Markets Desk that it was a co-lead manager of an aggressively priced five-year, Australian dollar (A$) zero-coupon issue which was selling very well in Europe. The London Syndicate believed it could successfully underwrite a similar five-year A$ zero-coupon issue for Kodak. It was determined that Merrill Lynch could meet Kodak's funding target if an attractively priced A$ zero-coupon swap could be found.

To meet Kodak's minimum issue size of U.S. $75 million, an A$ 200 million zero-coupon issue would be necessary, which was the largest A$ zero-coupon issue ever underwritten at that time. Merrill Lynch then received a firm mandate on a five-year A$ 130 million zero-coupon swap with Australian Bank B at a semi-annual interest rate of 13.39 percent. The remaining A$ 70 million was arranged through a long-dated forward foreign exchange contract with Australian Bank A at a forward rate of A$ 1 = U.S. $0.5286.

With the currency swap mandate and the long-dated forward contract, Merrill Lynch received final approval by Kodak for the transaction and the five-year A$ 200 million zero-coupon issue was launched in Europe at a net price of 54⅛ percent, with a gross spread of 1⅛ percent. Net proceeds to Kodak were 53 percent of A$ 200 million or A$ 106 million. Kodak converted this principal into U.S. $75 million at the spot rate of U.S. $0.7059. Simultaneously, Merrill Lynch entered into a currency swap with Kodak to convert the Australian dollar cash flows into U.S. dollar cash flows at 7.35 percent, paid semiannually, or U.S. Treasuries plus 35 basis points (since five-year Treasury bonds were then yielding approximately 7 percent). As part of this swap, Merrill Lynch agreed to make semi-annual interest payments of LIBOR less 40 basis points to Australian Bank B. Merrill Lynch then arranged an interest rate swap to convert a portion of the fixed-rate payments from Kodak into floating rate payments to Bank B. Figure 5–3 contains an annotated schematic diagram of the currency and interest rate swaps and the long-dated foreign exchange purchase that appeared in a Merrill Lynch advertisement. Table 5–4 summarizes the period-by-period cash flows associated with these transactions.

The final column of Table 5–4 presents the net cash flows to Merrill Lynch from these transactions. The net present value of these flows, discounted at r percent, compounded semi-annually, is

$$NPV = \sum_{t=1}^{10} \$968,250/(1 + r/2)^t$$

$$- \$10,000,000/(1 + r/2)^{10}$$

Discounted at the then risk-free, five-year Treasury bond rate of 7 percent, compounded semi-annually, the NPV of these flows is $963,365. Using a higher discount rate, say 7.5 percent, to reflect the various risks associated with these transactions, results in a net present value to Merrill Lynch of $1,031,826. The actual NPV of these cash flows falls somewhere in between these two extremes.

By combining a non-dollar issue with a currency swap and interest rate swap, Merrill Lynch was able to construct an innovative, lower-cost source of funds for Kodak. The entire package involved close teamwork and a complex set of transactions on three continents. In turn, through its willingness to consider nontraditional financing methods, Kodak was able to lower its cost of funds

Figure 5–3. A$200,000,000 Kodak Zero Coupon Eurobond and Currency Swap

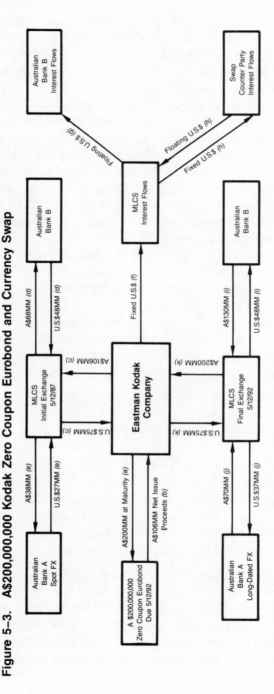

a. Investors receive a single payment of A$200 million on May 12, 1992, which represents both principal and interest.
b. The bonds are priced at 54⅜ less 1⅛ gross spread. Net proceeds to Kodak at settlement on May 12,1987, are A$106 million.
c. Kodak exchanges A$106,000,000 with MLCS and receives U.S. $75,000,000 at a fixed semi-annual interest rate of 7.35%.
d. Australian Bank B provides a 5-year A$130 million zero coupon swap at a semi-annual rate of 13.39%. In the currency swap's initial exchange on May 12, 1987, MLCS pays Australian Bank B A$68,000,000 (A$130,000,000 × [1/1 + (13.39%/2)]¹⁰]) and receives U.S. $48,000,000 (A$68,000,000 × .7059) based on a spot exchange rate of U.S. $0.7059/A$1.
e. MCLS sells the remaining A$38,000,000 (A$106,000,000 − A$68,000,000)) to Australian Bank A on May 12, 1992 at a spot rate of U.S. $.7105/A$1 and receives U.S. $27,000,000.
f. Kodak makes semi-annual fixed-rate interest payments of U.S. $2,756,250 to MLCS ((7.35%/2) × U.S. $75,000,000).
g. MLCS makes semi-annual floating-rate interest payments of LIBOR less 40 basis points on a notional principal amount of U.S. $48,000,000 to Australian Bank B.
h. MLCS make s semi-annual interest payments of U.S.$1,884,000, based on a notional principal amount of U.S.$48,000,000 and fixed interest rate of 7.85%, and receives semi-annual floating-rate interest payments of LIBOR flat in a fixed/floating interest rate swap with its book.
i. MLCS receives A$130 million and pays U.S.$48,000,000 in the Australian Bank B currency swap's final exchange on May 12, 1992.
j. In a long-dated forward foreign exchange transaction with Australian Bank A, MLCS purchases A$70 million on May 12, 1992, for U S.$37 million based on a forward exchange rate of U.S.$0.5286/A$1.
k. On May 12, 1992, Kodak pays U.S. $75,000,000 to MLCS, receives A$200,000,000 in return, and Kodak then pays the A$200,000,000 to its zero coupon bondholders.

Table 5-4. MLCS Cash Flows—Eastman Kodak Transaction

Date	Cash Flow Type	Kodak Currency Swap		Australian Bank B Currency Swap		Foreign Exchange Market		Fixed Floating US$ Swap		Net US$ Flows
		A$	US$	A$	US$	A$	US$	Fixed	Floating	
12 May 87	Initial Exchange	$106,000,000	($75,000,000)	($ 68,000,000)	$48,000,000	$38,000,000	$27,000,000	—	—	—
12 Nov. 87	Interest Flow	—	$2,756,250 (a)	—	(LIBOR—40BPS)	—	—	($1,884,000)(b)	LIBOR	$968,250(c)
12 May 88	Interest Flow	—	$2,756,250	—	(LIBOR—40BPS)	—	—	($1,884,000)	LIBOR	$968,250
12 May 88	Interest Flow	—	$2,756,250	—	(LIBOR—40BPS)	—	—	($1,884,000)	LIBOR	$968,250
12 May 89	Interest Flow	—	$2,756,250	—	(LIBOR—40BPS)	—	—	($1,884,000)	LIBOR	$968,250
12 Nov. 89	Interest Flow	—	$2,756,250	—	(LIBOR—40BPS)	—	—	($1,884,000)	LIBOR	$968,250
12 May 90	Interest Flow	—	$2,756,250	—	(LIBOR—40BPS)	—	—	($1,884,000)	LIBOR	$968,250
12 Nov. 90	Interest Flow	—	$2,756,250	—	(LIBOR—40BPS)	—	—	($1,884,000)	LIBOR	$968,250
12 May 91	Interest Flow	—	$2,756,250	—	(LIBOR—40BPS)	—	—	($1,884,000)	LIBOR	$968,250
12 Nov. 91	Interest Flow	—	$2,756,250	—	(LIBOR—40BPS)	—	—	($1,884,000)	LIBOR	$968,250
12 May 92	Interest Flow	—	$2,756,250	—	(LIBOR—40BPS)	—	—	($1,884,000)	LIBOR	$968,250
12 Nov. 92	Interest Flow	—	$2,756,250	—	(LIBOR—40BPS)	—	—	($1,884,000)	LIBOR	$968,250
12 May 92	Final Exchange	($200,000,000)	$75,000,000	$130,000,000	($48,000,000)	$70,000,000	($37,000,000)	($1,884,000)	LIBOR	($10,000,000)

a (US$75,000,000) × (.0735) × (180 days/360 days)

b (US$48,345,423) × (.0785) × (180 days/360 days)

c US$2,756,250 − US$1,884,000 + ((US$48,000,000 × .004 × (180 days/360 days)) by about 15 basis points, yielding an annual savings of approximately \$112,500 (.0015 × \$75,000,000). The present value of this savings, discounted at 7.5 percent compounded semi-annually is

$$PV = \sum_{t=1}^{10} 56,250/(1.0375)^t$$

$$= \$461,969$$

Economic Advantages of Swaps

For swaps to provide a real economic benefit to both parties, a barrier generally must exist to prevent arbitrage from functioning fully. This impediment must take the form of legal restrictions on spot and forward foreign exchange transactions, different perceptions by investors of risk and creditworthiness of the two parties, appeal or acceptability of one borrower to a certain class of investor, tax differentials, and so forth.[5]

Swaps also allow firms to lower their cost of foreign exchange risk management. A U.S. corporation, for example, may want to secure fixed-rate funds in deutsche marks in order to reduce its DM exposure but is hampered in doing so because it is a relatively unknown credit in the German financial market. In contrast, a German corporation well established in its own country but relatively unknown in the U.S. financial market may desire floating-rate dollar financing.

In such a case, a bank intermediary familiar with the funding needs and "comparative advantages" in borrowing of both parties may arrange a currency swap. The U.S. company borrows floating-rate dollars and the German company borrows fixed-rate DM. The two companies then swap both principal and interest payments. When the term of the swap matures, say, in five years, the principal amounts revert to the original holder. Both parties receive a cost savings because they borrow initially in the market where they have a comparative advantage and then swap for their preferred liability.

Currency swaps thus are often used to provide long-term financing in foreign currencies. This is an important function, since in many foreign countries, long-term capital and forward foreign exchange markets are notably absent or not well developed. Swaps are one vehicle providing liquidity to these markets.

In effect, swaps allow the transacting parties to engage in some form of tax, regulatory system, or financial market arbitrage. If the world capital market were fully integrated, the incentive to swap would be reduced because fewer arbitrage opportunities would exist. As noted above, however, even in the United States, where financial markets function freely, interest rate swaps are extremely popular and credited with cost savings.

Bank Loan Swaps

In recent years, a market has developed that enables investors to purchase the external debt of less developed countries (LDCs) to acquire equity or domestic currency in those same countries. The market for LDC debt swaps, as the transactions are called, has grown rapidly over the past few years. Between 1985, when swapping began, and 1987, about $5 billion worth of LDC loans were swapped. Although the rate at which debt swaps are occurring is still small in relation to the $437 billion that the fifteen most troubled debtor nations owe the world's commercial banks, there are indications that the debt swaps market is poised for faster growth. Six major debtor nations—Brazil, Chile, Mexico, Venezuela, Argentina, and the Philippines—have initiated debt swaps programs, and more will likely follow.

Types of Debt Swaps and Their Rationale

Debt swaps can be quite complex, but the basics are fairly simple. For several years, European and regional U.S. commercial banks have been selling troubled loans in the so-called secondary market. The loans trade at deep discounts to their face value, reflecting the market's opinion that they will not be repaid in full. For example, in mid-1987 Chilean debt sold at about 70 percent of its face value, or 70 cents on the dollar. Mexican loans traded at about 60 percent of par, Brazilian loans at 40 percent, and Bolivian debt at a mere 10 percent.

In a typical deal, a multinational that wants to invest in, say, Chile, hires a middleman (usually a bank) to buy Chilean loans in the secondary market. The company (again through a middleman) presents the loans, denominated in dollars, to the Chilean central bank, which redeems them for Chilean pesos. The central banks pay less than face value but more than the loans trade for in the secondary market. Chile pays about 92 cents on the dollar and Mexico an average of 88 cents.

Thus, a company that wants to expand in Chile can pick up $100 million of loans in the secondary market for $70 million and swap them for $92 million in pesos. Chile gets $100 million of debt off its books and does not have to part with precious dollars. The company gets $92 million of investment for $70 million, which amounts to a 24 percent subsidy (22/90).

The variations on this theme are endless. Chrysler has used some of the pesos it got in swaps to pay off local debt owed by its Mexican subsidiary. Kodak and Unisys have used swaps to expand their operations in Chile. Club Med is building a new beach resort in Mexico. Big U.S. banks usually act only as middlemen in these deals, but a few have swapped for themselves, trading their LDC loans for equity in Latin American businesses.

In addition to debt-equity swaps, there are also "debt-peso" swaps. Debt-peso swaps enable residents of a debtor country to purchase their country's foreign debt at a discount and to convert this debt into domestic currency. Residents use funds held abroad, or hard currency acquired from international trade or in the exchange market to finance these purchases.

By arrangement with the debt country, domestic currency assets obtained via debt swaps are acquired at closer to the original face value of the debt. For example, in 1986, a purchaser who acquired Mexican debt for 57 cents on the dollar could obtain equity worth 82 cents. Even after accounting for fees and redemption discounts applied by debtor countries to convert the debt into domestic currency, debt swaps allow investors to acquire the domestic currency of debtor countries much more cheaply than possible on official exchange markets. In effect, investors resorting to the debt swap market enjoy a preferential exchange rate.

Typically, access to swap programs involves wading through a lot of government red tape. For example, rules for foreign investors to participate in Mexico's swap program are outlined in sometimes indecipherable language in a forty-four page *Manual Operativo*.

Mexico also tailors its swap program to promote industrial policy goals; it does that by redeeming loans at different prices depending on how the proceeds will be used. If a foreign investor wants to buy shares in a nationalized company that the government is trying to privatize, the central bank redeems loans at full face value. It pays as much as 95 cents on the dollar if the pesos will be invested in tourism and other businesses that help the trade balance—but pays only 75 cents on the dollar on deals that create no jobs, no exports, and no new technology.

6

Designing a Global Financing Strategy

In selecting an appropriate strategy for financing its worldwide operations, the multinational firm must consider the availability of different sources of funds and their relative costs and effects on the firm's financial risks. Some of the key variables in the evaluation include the firm's capital structure (debt-equity mix), taxes, exchange risk, diversification of fund sources, the freedom to move funds across borders, and a variety of government credit and capital controls and subsidies. The eventual funding strategy selected must reconcile a variety of potentially conflicting objectives such as minimizing expected financing costs, reducing economic exposure, providing protection against currency controls and other forms of political risk, and assuring availability of funds in times of tight credit.

The choice of trade-offs to be made in establishing a worldwide financial policy requires an explicit analytical framework. The approach taken in this chapter divides the financing of international operations into three largely separable objectives:[1]

1. Minimize expected after-tax financing costs.
2. Arrange financing to reduce the riskiness of operating cash flows.
3. Achieve an appropriate worldwide financial structure.

Minimizing Expected After-Tax Financing Costs

Sharp-eyed firms are always on the lookout for financing choices that are "bargains"—that is, financing options priced at below-market rates. Bargains result from capital market distortions that grow out of tax asymmetries, government credit and capital controls, or subsidies designed to achieve goals other than economic efficiency.

Taxes

The asymmetrical tax treatment of various components of financial cost such as dividend payments versus interest expenses, and exchange losses versus exchange gains holds out the possibility of reducing after-tax costs by judicious selection of securities. Yet everything is not always what it seems.

For example, many firms consider debt financing to be less expensive than equity financing, because interest expense is tax deductible whereas dividends are not. But this comparison is too limited. In the absence of any restrictions, the supply of corporate debt could be expected to rise. Yields would have to rise also in order to attract investors in ever higher tax brackets. Companies would continue to issue debt up to the point at which the marginal investor tax rate would equal the marginal corporate tax rate.[2] At this point, the necessary yield would be such that there would no longer be a tax incentive for issuing more debt.

The tax advantage of debt can be preserved only if the firm can take advantage of some tax distortion, issue tax-exempt debt, or sell debt to investors in marginal tax brackets below 34 percent. Examples of debt in the respective categories are bonds denominated in weak currencies, zero-coupon bonds, and bearer bonds.

Choice of Currency

International interest arbitrage implies that, holding risk constant, the nominal yield differential between debt denominated in different currencies should equal the expected change in the exchange rate during the term of the loan. In the presence of taxes, however, this is not necessarily the case. For example, if arbitrage equilibrates real yields before tax, then the classic corporate prescription to issue weak-currency debt will minimize expected after-tax financing costs.[3]

Zero-Coupon Bonds

In 1982, the first zero-coupon bond was issued. Zero-coupon bonds (or "zeros") pay no interest, but are sold at a deep discount to their face value. Investors gain from the difference between the discounted price and the amount they receive at redemption.

Since 1982, investors worldwide have paid $4 billion for $18.9 billion worth of zero-coupon bonds. About one-half of these have been purchased by Japanese investors. The offerings are attractive in Japan because the government does not tax the capital gain on bonds sold prior to maturity. Catering to this tax break, a number of U.S. companies—including Exxon and IBM—obtained inexpensive financing by targeting Japanese investors for zero-coupon Eurobonds.

The value of being able to take quick advantage of such tax windows is evident considering subsequent developments in Japan. Japan's Finance Ministry, embarrassed at this tax break, in 1982 first banned the sale of any new zero-coupon bonds in Japan. About a year later, it reversed itself and permitted zeros to be sold, with various restrictions. In early 1985, the Finance Ministry decided unofficially to tax the bonds, although the exact form this tax will take, should it be instituted, is unresolved as of this writing. But the tax is bad news to U.S. corporate issuers, because Japanese investors demand to be compensated for their possible tax liability.

Bearer Bonds

The bearer bond was designed with investor tax concerns in mind. Unlike ordinary securities, which must be registered in the name of the purchaser, bearer bonds are unregistered. This feature allows investors to collect interest in complete anonymity and thereby evade taxes. Although U.S. law prohibits the sale of such bonds to American citizens or residents, bonds issued in bearer form are not illegal overseas. As expected, investors are willing to accept lower yields on bearer bonds than on nonbearer bonds of comparable risk.

American firms have long been able to reduce their cost of funds by selling bearer bonds abroad. But prior to 1984, the United States imposed a 30 percent withholding tax on interest paid to foreign investors, largely negating the benefits of issuing bearer bonds. To accommodate foreign investors, U.S. firms raising money abroad issued securities through offshore finance subsidiaries, thereby making interest payments by the finance subsidiary to foreign investors exempt from U.S. withholding tax. The Netherlands Antilles (N.A.) was a particularly attractive location for such a venture, because a bilateral tax treaty between the United States and the N.A. exempts interest payments by the parent to its N.A. finance subsidiary from U.S. withholding tax.

The combination of bearer form and exemption from U.S. withholding taxes meant that highly rated American companies could issue Eurobonds at rates considerably below the coupon rates equivalent securities would carry when issued in the United States. Often corporations could borrow abroad below the cost at which the U.S. government borrowed domestically. As a result, use of offshore finance subsidiaries grew rapidly; in 1982 and 1983, some $20 billion of Eurobonds were issued by U.S. companies. The pace accelerated when the Tax Act of 1984 repealed the withholding tax on dividend and interest payments to foreign citizens, enabling American firms to sell bearer bonds overseas directly. American firms sold $20 billion of new issues in the Eurobond market in 1984 alone.

Debt Versus Equity Financing

Interest payments on debt, extended by either the parent or a financial institution, generally are tax deductible by an affiliate, but dividends are not. In addition, principal repatriation is tax free, whereas dividend payments may lead to further taxation. Thus, parent company financing of foreign affiliates in the form of debt rather than equity has certain tax advantages.

Government Credit and Capital Controls

Governments often intervene in their financial markets to achieve goals other than economic efficiency. For example, a government might limit corporate borrowing to hold down interest rates, thereby providing its finance ministry with a lower-cost source of funds to meet a budget deficit. Or the government might attempt to control balance-of-payments deficits by restricting overseas investment flows, as the United States did from 1968 to 1974 under the Office of Foreign Direct Investment regulations.

When access to local funds markets is limited, interest rates in those markets are usually below the risk-adjusted equilibrium level. The MNC, with access to a variety of sources and types of funds, plus the ability to shift capital with its internal transfer system, has more opportunities to secure the lowest risk-adjusted cost of money and to circumvent credit restraints. These attributes should give it a substantial advantage compared over a purely domestic company.

Government Subsidies and Incentives

Most governments offer a variety of incentives to influence production and export sourcing decisions. For example, investments located in the Mezzogiorno region of Italy can qualify for cash grants that cover up to 40 percent of the cost of plant and equipment, in addition to subsidized loans and other investment incentives. Governments sometimes make the infrastructure investments as well, thereby providing the base to support a new industrial project.

In addition, governments of most developed nations attempt to provide their domestic exporters with a competitive edge in the form of low-cost export financing and concessionary rates on political and economic risk insurance. The U.S. government, for example, supplies low-cost export credits through the Export-Import Bank (Ex-Im Bank).

These export credit programs often can be used to advantage by multinational firms. The form of use will depend on whether the firm is seeking to export or import goods or services, but the basic strategy remains the same: Shop around among the various export credit agencies for the best possible financing arrangement.

Cross Company, for example, had $40 million of machine tool orders in 1982 from a Ford Motor Company unit in Mexico. Cross wanted to put the orders through its Michigan factory. But the British government was willing to provide less expensive export financing than the Ex-Im Bank, so the Cross plant in England got the order.

Firms engaged in projects with sizable import requirements may be able to finance these purchases on attractive terms from various export financing agencies. To do this, the firm must compile a list of goods and services required for the project and relate them to potential sources by country. Where there is overlap among potential suppliers, the purchaser may be able to extract more favorable financing terms from the export credit agencies involved. Perhaps the best-known application of this strategy in recent years is the financing of the Soviet gas pipeline to Western Europe. By playing off the European and Japanese export financing agencies against each other, the Soviet Union managed to get very favorable credit terms.

Regional and International Development Banks

Organizations such as the World Bank and Inter-American Development Bank are potential sources of low-cost, long-term, fixed-rate funds for certain types of ventures. The time-consuming nature of arranging financing from them, however, due in part to their insistence on conducting their own in-house feasibility studies, usually leaves them as a secondary source of funds. Their participation may be indispensable, however, for projects that require heavy infrastructure investments such as roads, power plants, schools, communications facilities, and housing for employees. These infrastructure investments are the most difficult part of a project for which to arrange financing because they generate no cash flow of their own. Thus, loans or grants from an international or regional development bank are often essential to fill a gap in the project financing plan.

Reducing Operating Risks

After a firm has taken advantage of the opportunities available to lower its risk-adjusted financing costs, it then should arrange its additional financing in such a way that operating risks are reduced. The profitability, and thus the market value, of any company depends to a large extent on its ability to compete. A key element of corporate competitiveness is the firm's ability to inspire sufficient trust and confidence such that customers, employees, and other stakeholders are willing to develop relationships with the firm. One prerequisite for such confidence is that the firm be seen as financially sound and viable over the long run.

Clearly, excessive risk taking—with a corresponding decrease in the firm's survival odds—could adversely affect the firm's relationships with its non-investor stakeholders, thereby jeopardizing the firm-specific capital that has been accumulated over time. The result, as seen earlier, is that higher total risk can lead to a reduction in a company's operating cash flows by decreasing sales or increasing operating costs.[4]

Thus, to the extent that a particular element of risk contributes materially to the firm's total risk, management will want to lay off that risk as long as the cost of doing so is not too great. The risks and their relationship to financing arrangements examined here arise from four sources: currency fluctuations, political instability, sales uncertainty, and changing access to funds.

Since the political and economic changes that bring about these risks are impossible to predict—otherwise there would be no risk—the firm cannot expect to profit from financial arrangements that lay such risks off to others. Rather, these financial arrangements should be viewed as insurance against corporate risk.

Exchange Risk
Earlier it was seen how firms can structure their liabilities in such a way as to minimize their exposure to exchange risk. Essentially, this involves financing assets that generate foreign currency cash flows, with liabilities denominated in those same foreign currencies, with the goal being to offset unanticipated changes in the home currency value of operating cash flows with identical changes in the home currency cost of servicing its liabilities. While a perfect hedge is not possible because of uncertainty, the hedging objective at least provides a clear-cut goal for firms.

Political Risk
The use of financing to reduce political risks typically involves mechanisms to avoid or at least reduce the impact of certain risks, such as those of exchange convertibility. It also may involve financing mechanisms that actually change the risk itself, as in the case of expropriation or other direct political acts.

Firms sometimes can reduce the risk of currency inconvertibility by appropriately arranging their affiliates' financing. This includes investing parent funds as debt rather than equity, arranging back-to-back and parallel loans, and using local financing to the maximum extent possible. Of course, such arrangements will be most valuable when the banks or local investors face significantly fewer restrictions or smaller risks—especially if the risk in question involves possible discrimination against direct foreign investors. While local investors often may have an advantage in this regard, this is not a general rule. Even if a particular political risk cannot be modified by shifting it from one firm or investor to another, a firm with substantial exposure will benefit by laying off such risks to investors with less exposure.

Another approach used by MNCs, especially those in the extractive industries, is financing their foreign investments with funds from the host and other governments, international development agencies, overseas banks, or even from customers, rather than supplying their own capital. Because repayment is tied to the project's success, the firms sponsoring the project can create an international network of banks, government agencies, and customers with a vested interest in the fulfillment of the host government's contract with the sponsoring firms. This strategy was used successfully by Kennecott to finance a major copper mine expansion in Chile. Despite the subsequent rise to power of Salvador Allende, who promised to expropriate all foreign holdings in Chile with "ni un centavo" ("not one cent") in compensation, the Chilean government was forced to honor all its prior commitments to Kennecott.

International leasing is another financing technique that may help multinationals reduce their political risk. It allows multinationals to limit the ownership of assets by subsidiaries in politically unstable countries and to more easily extract cash from affiliates located in countries where there are exchange controls.

Product Market Risk

Some firms sell their project's or plant's expected output in advance to their customers on the basis of mutual advantage. The purchaser benefits from these so-called "take-or-pay" contracts by having a stable source of supply, usually at a discount from the market price. The seller also benefits by having an assured outlet for its product, which protects the firm against the risk of demand fluctuations, as well as a contract that it can then discount with a consortium of banks. This technique was used to help finance Kennecott's Chilean copper mine expansion and the Soviet Union's natural gas pipeline to Western Europe.

Securing Access to Funds

A firm's operational flexibility depends partly on its ability to secure continual access to funds at a reasonable cost and without onerous restrictions. This allows the firm to meet temporary cash shortfalls as well as to take advantage of profitable investment opportunities without having to sell off assets or otherwise disrupt operations. The fear is that during some future period of monetary stringency, the quantity of credit available to it might be limited, while its competitors still retained access to funds in a broader range of markets. In such conditions of uneven credit allocation, the market shares of the firm's own business would be at risk, since the scale of its operations would be limited by the scale of available finance. This potential problem creates demand among firms for access to an expanded range of credit sources.

The ability to marshall substantial financial resources also signals competitors, actual and potential, that the firm will not be an easy target. Consider the alternative—a firm that is highly leveraged, with no excess lines of credit, or cash reserves. A competitor can move into the firm's market and gain market share with less fear of retaliation. In order to retaliate—by cutting price, say, or by increasing advertising expenditures—the firm will need more money. Since it has no spare cash and cannot issue additional debt at a reasonable price, it will have to go to the equity market. But firms issuing new equity are suspect because of the asymmetric information relationship between investors and management (is the firm selling equity now because it knows the stock is overpriced?). The problem of information asymmetry will be particularly acute when the firm is trying to fend off a competitive attack. Thus, a firm that lacks financial reserves faces a Hobson's choice: Acquiesce in the competitive attack or raise funds on unattractive terms.

To ensure adequate financial reserves, an MNC can maintain substantial unused debt capacity and liquid assets. It can also diversify its fund sources and indirectly buy insurance through excess borrowing. Having these extra financial resources signals competitors, as well as customers and other stakeholders, that the firm is financially healthy and has staying power; temporary setbacks will not become permanent ones.

Diversification of Fund Sources

A key element of corporate financial strategy should be to gain access to a broad range of fund sources to lessen a company's dependence on any one financial market. A further benefit is that the firm broadens its sources of economic and financial information, aiding in its financial decisionmaking.

According to Natomas, the San Francisco-based oil producer, it sold a $30 million Eurobond issue in 1977 even though it could have obtained funds at a lower cost from American banks. The key purpose of raising funds abroad was to introduce the company's name to international investors as part of its global financial strategy.[5] By floating a Eurobond, the firm was able to make the acquaintance of some of the largest non-American financial institutions in the world, including Swiss Bank Corporation, the issue's lead manager. In addition, these European institutions were expected to serve Natomas as a source of market and economic information to counterbalance the input it was receiving already from U.S. banks.

The threat of domestic credit controls has accelerated the trend toward global diversification of financing sources. For example, after the Federal Reserve Board tightened credit in October 1979 and proposed a voluntary ceiling on loan growth in March 1980, many anxious corporate treasurers feared that mandatory credit controls might be close at hand. Large numbers of them then arranged to borrow abroad, far from the Fed's reach.

Excess Borrowing

Most firms have lines of credit with a number of banks that give them the right to borrow up to an agreed-upon credit limit. Unused balances carry an annual commitment fee, normally on the order of 0.5 percent. In order not to tie up funds unnecessarily, most banks periodically review each credit limit to see whether the customer's account activity level justifies that credit line. Some firms are willing to borrow funds that they do not require (and then place them on deposit elsewhere) in order to maintain their credit limit in the event of a tight money situation. In effect, they are buying insurance against the possibility of being out of the money market. One measure of the cost of this policy is the difference between the borrowing rate and the deposit rate, multiplied by the average amount of borrowed funds placed on deposit. Another cost may be considerable banker ill will if a corporation borrows when money is tight and does not use the money "productively."

Establishing a Worldwide Financial Structure

A problem that has long perplexed financial executives of multinational corporations is how to arrange the capital structures of their foreign affiliates and what factors are relevant in making this decision. Specifically, the problem is whether financial structures should

1. conform to that of the parent company;
2. reflect the capitalization norms in each foreign country; or
3. vary so as to take advantage of opportunities to minimize taxes, offset risks, or exploit distortions in financial markets.

Disregarding public and government relations and legal requirements for the moment, the parent company could finance its foreign affiliates by raising funds in its own country and investing these funds as equity. The overseas operations would then have a zero debt ratio. Alternatively, the parent could hold only one dollar of share capital in each affiliate and require all to borrow on their own, with or without guarantees; in this case, affiliate debt ratios would approach 100 percent. Or the parent could borrow itself and invest these funds in the form of debt. Here again, the affiliates' debt ratios would be close to 100 percent. In all these cases, the total amount of borrowing and the debt-equity mix of the consolidated corporation are identical. Thus, the question of an optimal capital structure for a foreign affiliate is completely distinct from the corporation's overall debt-equity ratio.

Moreover, any accounting rendition of a separate capital structure for the subsidiary is illusory *unless* the parent is willing to allow its affiliate to default on its debt.[6] As long as the rest of the MNC group has a legal or moral obligation or sound business reasons for preventing the affiliate from defaulting, the individual unit has no independent capital structure. Rather, its true debt ratio is equal to that of the consolidated group.

Some evidence on parent willingness to guarantee (implicitly, if not explicitly) their affiliates' debts is provided by two surveys. Robert Stobaugh reported that not one of a sample of twenty medium and large multinationals (average annual foreign sales of $200 million and $1 billion, respectively) said it would allow its subsidiaries to default on debt that did not have a parent company guarantee.[7] Of the small multinationals interviewed (average annual foreign sales of $50 million), only one out of seventeen indicated that it might allow a subsidiary to default on its obligations.

A survey by Business International of eight U.S.-based MNCs had similar findings.[8] The majority of firms surveyed said they would make good the nonguaranteed debt of a subsidiary in the event of a default. Moreover, most of the firms expressed little concern with the debt-equity mixes of their foreign affiliates. Their primary focus was on worldwide, rather than individual, capital structure.

The third option, therefore, to vary affiliate financial structures to take advantage of local financing opportunities, appears to be the best choice. Thus, within the constraints set by foreign statutory or minimum equity requirements, the need to appear to be a responsible and good guest, and the requirements of a worldwide financial structure, an MNC should finance its affiliates to best exploit the special opportunities of being multinational.

The choice of where to borrow to finance foreign operations has become more complicated with passage of the Tax Reform Act of 1986 since the distribution of debt between U.S. parents and their foreign subsidiaries affects the use of foreign tax credits. Many U.S.-based MNCs are now in an excess foreign tax credit (FTC) position. One approach to using up these FTCs is to push expenses overseas—and thus lower overseas profits—by increasing the leverage of foreign subsidiaries. In the aforementioned example, the U.S. parent may have one of its taxpaying foreign units borrow funds and ship these funds back to the parent as a dividend. The parent can then turn around and invest these funds as equity in the non-taxpaying subsidiary. In this way, the worldwide corporation can reduce its taxes without being subject to the constraints imposed by the Tax Reform Act.

As an alternative to increasing the debt of foreign subsidiaries, American multinationals could expand their use of leasing in the United States. Although leasing an asset is economically equivalent to using borrowed funds to purchase the asset, the international tax consequences differ. Prior to 1986, American multinationals counted virtually all their interest expense as a fully deductible U.S. expense. Under the new law, firms must allocate interest expense on general borrowings to match the location of their assets, even if all the interest is paid in the United States. This new rule reduces the amount of interest expense that can be written off against U.S. income. Rental expense, on the other hand, now can be allocated to the location of the leased property. Lease payments on equipment located in the United States, therefore, can be fully deducted.

At the same time, leasing equipment to be used in the United States, instead of borrowing to finance it, increases a firm's reported foreign income (since there is less interest expense to allocate against foreign income). The effect of leasing, therefore, is to increase the allowable foreign tax credit to offset U.S. taxes owed on foreign source income. This provides another tax advantage of leasing for firms that owe U.S. tax on their foreign source income.

7

Summary and Conclusions

The purpose of this book has been to develop financial policies that are appropriate for a multinational firm. To do this, it was necessary to internationalize the conceptual framework that has proven so valuable in matters of domestic corporate finance. The basic financial principles on which this framework rests can be summarized easily: More wealth is preferred to less wealth; sooner is better than later; and less risk is preferred to more risk. All the conclusions that have come to be recognized as key to analyzing corporate financial policies—what matters is not the quantity of money per se but the purchasing power represented by that money; investors will only pay for value received; one cannot expect to profit from or successfully protect against expected changes; and managers and investors respond in a rational manner, on average, to the economic incentives, opportunities, and information they face—are logically derived consequences of the rational pursuit of economic self-interest, based on the above three principles.

The application of these basic principles to international finance leads to a simple, yet elegant, set of equilibrium relationships that should hold among product prices, interest rates, and spot and forward exchange rates if there is no tampering with markets. Based on these parity conditions, which include purchasing power parity, interest rate parity, and the Fisher and international Fisher effects, and the hypothesis that investors focus on corporate cash flows, not reported accounting profits, the consequences of exchange rate changes for the value of the firm were analyzed.

It was concluded that the accounting profession's focus on the balance sheet impact of currency changes is misplaced: What matters is the effect that these changes may have on future cash flows. It became apparent that currency risk and inflation risk are intertwined; that through the theory of purchasing power parity, these risks are largely offsetting. One implication is that, in order to measure exposure properly, we must focus on inflation-adjusted or real exchange rates instead of nominal or actual exchange rates.

Next the management of exchange risk was discussed. Firms normally cope with anticipated currency changes by engaging in a variety of hedging activities. However, in normal circumstances, hedging cannot provide protection against expected exchange rate changes. The reason is that profits from hedging must come at the expense of the other party to the hedge, which is equally determined to profit. The cost of hedging, therefore, will adjust to reflect expected exchange rate changes. Thus, the basic value of hedging is to protect a company against unexpected exchange rate changes, which, by definition, are unpredictable and consequently, from which it is impossible to expect to profit. The existence of two profit-seeking parties to any currency transaction also suggests the likely futility of profitably forecasting exchange rates.

As currency risk affects all facets of a firm's operations, the key to effective exchange risk management is to factor currency considerations into all operational decisions, where warranted. Operating managers, in particular, should concentrate their efforts on the marketing and production initiatives that will be necessary to ensure and increase profitability in the long run. They should develop proactive, rather than reactive, strategic alternatives in order to gain competitive leverage internationally.

The effects of exchange rate changes and inflation also must be factored into working capital management in the MNC. Despite conceptual similarities in managing working capital in both the domestic and multinational firm, the complexity of having to deal with multiple money markets, currency fluctuations, exchange controls, and tax jurisdictions is likely to increase the payoffs from a knowledgeable and sophisticated approach to internationalizing the traditional components of working capital management.

Foreign investment analysis is another area likely to yield rich rewards upon the application of an appropriate methodology. The recommended approach is to estimate the incremental cash flows associated with an overseas project by means of a three-stage analysis. In the first stage, project cash flows are computed from the subsidiary's standpoint. The second stage involves calculating the project cash flows received by the parent company. This stage requires specific forecasts of the amounts, timing, and tax and other costs of transfers of project cash flows to headquarters. Finally, the firm must take into account the indirect benefits and costs that this investment confers on the rest of the system. For example, building a plant overseas might cannibalize or add to the export sales of another affiliate. In general, incremental cash flows can be found only by subtracting worldwide parent company cash flows in the investment's absence from postinvestment parent company cash flows.

Political and economic risks generally should be recognized by adjusting projected cash flows to reflect the expected impact of these risks, rather than by changing the discount rate. Cash flow adjustments are preferred on the pragmatic grounds that more and better information is available on the effect of such risks on future cash flows than on the required discount rate. In addition, adjusting a project's required rate of return to reflect incremental risk usually does not permit adequate consideration of the time pattern and magnitude of the risk being evaluated. The theoretical ground for avoiding discount rate adjustments is that the risks involved are generally unsystematic in nature and therefore, according to the capital asset pricing model, should not be priced.

The key point of the section on political risk in Chapter 4 is that many of these risks are controllable, given that appropriate policies are followed. Essentially, these policies involve structuring investments in such a way as to raise the cost to the host government of tampering with the investments. The anticipated results of these policies would then be reassessed in light of the capital budgeting framework presented earlier.

With regard to the impact of foreign operations on firm riskiness, analysis of the available evidence suggests that if there is an effect, it is generally to reduce both actual and perceived riskiness. These results indicate that at the very least, executives of multinational firms should seriously question the use of a risk premium to account for the added economic and political risks of overseas operations when evaluating prospective foreign investments.

Underlying the development of a successful program for investing overseas must be a corporate strategy that can create value for the firm's shareholders. The key to the development of such a strategy is to understand and then capitalize on those factors that led to success in the past. These factors generally take the form of a variety of firm-specific competitive advantages—including managerial skills, knowledge, and reputation for quality products and reliable service—that are difficult or expensive to sell apart from the firm's goods. To overcome these costs, many firms have created an internal market, one in which these firm-specific advantages can be embodied in the services and products they sell.

The process involved in searching for and utilizing those sources of differential advantage is clearly a difficult one. Essentially, it involves the establishment of suitable corporate objectives and policies, along with an inventory of corporate resources. These objectives, policies, and resources must be congruent with each other and must lead to the continual development of new sources of differential advantage as the older ones diminish in value.

In financing the foreign investments dictated by its corporate strategy, the multinational firm must take into account the wider choice of capital sources, the prevalence of government intervention in national capital markets, the large disparity in tax rates among nations, the existence of currency fluctuations and controls, and the ever-present possibility of political risks such as currency controls and expropriation. For the firm to do this, a three-stage framework is recommended. The primary emphasis is on taking advantage of distortions resulting from government intervention in financial markets or from different national tax laws, either of which may cause the after-tax costs of different sources and types of funds to differ. Secondarily, this framework includes the possibility of reducing various operating risks resulting from political or economic factors. Lastly, it seeks to determine appropriate parent, affiliate, and worldwide capital structures, taking into account the unique attributes of a multinational corporation.

Notes

Note: All multiple citations are listed in order of their publication dates.

Chapter 1: Introduction

1. The bases of the CAPM were provided by Harry Markowitz, *Portfolio Selection: Efficient Diversification of Investments* (New York: John Wiley & Sons, 1959); William F. Sharpe, "Capital Asset Prices: A Theory of Market Equilibrium Under Conditions of Risk," *Journal of Finance* (September 1964): 425–42; John Lintner, "The Valuation of Risk Assets and the Selection of Risky Investments in Stock Portfolios and Capital Budgets," *Review of Economics and Statistics* (February 1965): 13–37; and Jan Mossin, "Equilibrium in a Capital Asset Market," *Econometrica* (October 1966): 768–83. The formal theory of arbitrage pricing was first developed in Stephen A. Ross, "The Arbitrage Theory of Capital Asset Pricing," *Journal of Economic Theory* (December 1976): 341–60.

2. The rationale for taking total risk into account is elaborated on in Alan C. Shapiro and Sheridan Titman, "An Integrated Approach to Corporate Risk Management," *Midland Corporate Finance Journal* (Summer 1985): 41–56. Also see Gunter Dufey and Sam L. Srinivasulu, "The Case for Corporate Management of Foreign Exchange Risk," *Financial Management* (Summer 1984): 54–62.

Chapter 2: Foreign Exchange Risk Management

1. Surveys of the evidence and meanings of purchasing power parity can be found in Lawrence H. Officer, "The Purchasing-Power-Parity Theory of Exchange Rates: A Review Article," *IMF Staff Papers* (March 1976): 1–60; and Alan C. Shapiro, "What Does Purchasing Power Parity Mean?" *Journal of International Money and Finance* (December 1983): 295–318.

2. Evidence on the Fisher effect is provided in Eugene F. Fama, "Short-Term Interest Rates as Predictors of Inflation," *American Economic Review* (June 1975): 269–82. The international Fisher effect is evaluated in Ian H. Giddy and Gunter Dufey, "The Random Behavior of Flexible Exchange Rates," *Journal of International Business Studies* (Spring 1975): 1–32.

3. See, for example, Giddy and Dufey, "The Random Behavior of Flexible Exchange Rates," and Bradford Cornell, "Spot Rates, Forward Rates, and Market Efficiency," *Journal of Financial Economics* (1977): 55–65.

4. These criteria were suggested by Giddy and Dufey, "The Random Behavior of Flexible Exchange Rates."

5. Richard M. Levich, "Analyzing the Accuracy of Foreign Exchange Advisory Services: Theory and Evidence," in Richard Levich and Clas Wihlborg, eds., *Exchange Risk and Exposure* (Lexington, Mass.: D.C. Heath, 1980).

6. This section relies heavily on Chapters 9–11 in Alan C. Shapiro, *Multinational Financial Management*, 2nd edition (Boston: Allyn and Bacon, 1986); and Bradford Cornell and Alan C. Shapiro, "Managing Foreign Exchange Risks," *Midland Corporate Finance Journal* (Fall 1983): 16–31.

7. Current translation requirements are contained in Financial Accounting Standards Board, *Statement of Financial Accounting Standards No. 52* (Stamford, Conn.: Financial Accounting Standards Board, December 1981).

8. This section is based on C. Kent Garner and Alan C. Shapiro, "A Practical Method of Assessing Foreign Exchange Risk," *Midland Corporate Finance Journal* (Fall 1984): 6–17, which also illustrates the application of this method to an actual company. The theory underlying the method presented here is described

in Bernard Dumas, "The Theory of the Trading Firm Revisited," *Journal of Finance* (June 1978): 1014–29; and Alan C. Shapiro, "Currency Risk and Relative Price Risk," *Journal of Financial and Quantitative Analysis* (December 1984): 365–73.

9. Richard Roll, "Violations of the Law of One Price and Their Implications for Differentially-Denominated Assets," in Marshall Sarnat and George Szego, eds., *International Finance and Trade*, Vol. 1. (Cambridge, Mass.: Ballinger, 1979).

10. For more information on currency risk sharing, see Sam Srinivasulu and Edward Massura, "Sharing Currency Risks in Long-Term Contracts," *Business International Money Reports*, 23 February 1987.

11. For elaboration see Ian H. Giddy, "The Foreign Exchange Options as a Hedging Tool," *Midland Corporate Finance Journal* (Fall 1983): 32–42.

12. Gunter Dufey, "Corporate Financial Policies and Floating Exchange Rates," address presented at a meeting of the International Fiscal Association, Rome, October 14, 1974.

13. This section is based on Alan C. Shapiro and Thomas S. Robertson, "Managing Foreign Exchange Risks: The Role of Marketing Strategy," working paper, University of Pennsylvania, 1976.

14. Raymond Vernon, *Sovereignty at Bay* (New York: Basic Books, 1971).

15. This survey is reported on in *Fortune*, 26 November 1984.

16. *Wall Street Journal*, 10 August 1971.

Chapter 3: International Working Capital Management

1. See more information on multilateral payments netting in Alan C. Shapiro, "Payments Netting in International Cash Management," *Journal of International Business Studies* (Fall 1978): 51–58.

2. These possible objectives are suggested by Donald R. Lessard, "Currency and Tax Considerations in International Financing," Teaching Note No. 3, MIT, Spring 1979.

3. This section draws on material in Alan C. Shapiro, "Evaluating Financing Costs for Multinational Subsidiaries," *Journal of International Business Studies* (Fall 1975): 25–32.

4. Donald R. Lessard, "Transfer Prices, Taxes, and Financial Markets: Implications of Internal Financial Transfers Within the Multinational Firm," in Robert G. Hawkins, ed., *The Economic Effects of Multinational Corporations* (Greenwich, Conn.: JAI Press, 1979).

5. David P. Rutenberg, "Maneuvering Liquid Assets in a Multinational Company," *Management Science* (June 1970): B-671–84.

6. This section draws heavily on Donald R. Lessard, "Transfer Prices, Taxes, and Financial Markets."

7. Sidney M. Robbins and Robert B. Stobaugh, *Money in the Multinational Enterprise* (New York: Basic Books, 1973).

Chapter 4: Foreign Investment Analysis

1. The APV approach was developed by Stewart Myers, "Interactions of Corporate Financing and Investment Decisions," *Journal of Finance* (March 1974): 1–26.

2. The extension of the APV approach to foreign project appraisals is presented in Donald R. Lessard, "Evaluating Foreign Projects: An Adjusted Present Value Approach," in Donald R. Lessard, ed., *International Financial Management* (Boston: Warren, Gorham & Lamont, 1979).

3. W. Carl Kester, "Today's Options for Tomorrow's Growth," *Harvard Business Review* (March-April 1984): 153–60.

4. The notion of growth options for multinational firms is discussed in Carliss Baldwin, "Competing for Capital in a Global Environment," *Midland Corporate Finance Journal* (Spring 1987): 43–64.

5. The material in this section is elaborated on in Alan C. Shapiro, "Capital Budgeting for the Multinational Corporation," *Financial Management* (Spring 1978): 7–16.

6. Donald R. Lessard, "Evaluating Foreign Projects: An Adjusted Present Value Approach," in Donald R. Lessard, ed., *International Financial Management* (Boston: Warren, Gorham & Lamont, 1979).

7. For proof of this assertion, see Chapter 14 in Alan C. Shapiro, *Multinational Financial Management*, 2nd edition (Boston: Allyn and Bacon, 1986).

8. See, for example, studies by J. Frederick Truitt, "Expropriation of Foreign Investment: Summary of the Post–World War II Experience of American and British Investors in Less Developed Countries," *Journal of International Business Studies* (Fall 1970): 3–15; and David Bradley, "Managing Against Expropriation," *Harvard Business Review* (July-August 1977): 75–83.

9. See Bradley, "Managing Against Expropriation."

10. Arvind Mahajan, "Pricing Risk of Expropriation," working paper, 1988.

11. This strategy is elaborated on in Alan C. Shapiro, "Managing Political Risk: A Policy Approach," *Columbia Journal of World Business* (Fall 1981): 63–70.

12. A coherent strategy is presented in Alan C. Shapiro, "Managing Against Currency Controls," working paper, University of Southern California, 1980.

13. In the event of an expropriation, the expected return is not likely to be zero. Thus, it is also necessary to estimate the expected value of the net compensation provided in such a case. While difficult to foresee with any precision, such post-expropriation compensation can be expected to come from several sources:

    1. Direct compensation paid to the firm by the local government.
    2. Indirect compensation such as the management contracts received by oil companies whose properties were nationalized by the Venezuelan government.
    3. Payment received from political risk insurance.
    4. Tax deductions in the home country associated with such an extraordinary loss.
    5. A reduction in the amount of capital that must be repaid by the project equal to the unamortized portion of any local borrowing. It is inconceivable that a firm with an expropriated foreign operation would pay back any local borrowing except as part of a total compensation package worked out with the government.

14. Specifically, beta equals $cov(R_i, R_m)/var(R_m)$, where $cov(R_i, R_m)$ is the covariance between returns on investment i and returns on the market portfolio and $var(R_m)$ is the variance of returns on the market portfolio.

15. Donald R. Lessard, "World, Country, and Industry Relationships in Equity Returns: Implications for Risk Reduction Through International Diversification," *Financial Analysts Journal* (January-February 1976): 32–38.

16. Bruno Solnik, "Why Not Diversify Internationally Rather Than Domestically?" *Financial Analysts Journal* (July-August 1974): 48–54.

17. These barriers to international portfolio diversification are described at length in Gunter Dufey, "The Structure of Private Foreign Investment with Specific Reference to Portfolio Investment," Report prepared for U.S. Department of Treasury, OASIA/Research, January 31, 1976.

18. Ali M. Fatemi, "Shareholder Benefits from Corporate International Diversification," *Journal of Finance* (December 1984): 1325–44.

19. See, for example, Benjamin I. Cohen, *Multinational Firms and Asian Exports* (New Haven: Yale University Press, 1975); and Alan Rugman, "Risk Reduction by International Diversification," *Journal of International Business Studies* (Fall 1976): 75–80.

20. This section is elaborated on in Chapter 13 in Shapiro, *Multinational Financial Management*.

21. Richard E. Caves, "International Corporations: The Industrial Economics of Foreign Investment," *Economica* (February 1971): 1–27.

22. A study by The Conference Board, for instance, showed that 62 percent of the firms surveyed made no attempt to determine the net profits from their foreign licensing agreements. They treated these agreements as a free good, ignoring the opportunity costs that would have been revealed by a comparison of alternatives. Similarly, a survey by David Rutenberg of 120 companies disclosed that on average these companies accepted only about 11 percent of the joint venture proposals they received— rejecting 83 percent out of hand. Moreover, only one-third had a policy of actively searching for joint venture opportunities.

23. For an excellent discussion of Japanese strategy in the U.S. TV market and elsewhere see Gary Hamel and C.K. Prahalad, "Do You Really Have a Global Strategy?" *Harvard Business Review* (July-August 1985): 139–48.

Chapter 5: Financing Foreign Operations

1. A good discussion of the changing pattern of corporate financing is contained in "Corporate Finance: Topsy Turvy," *The Economist*, 7 June 1986.

2. Gordon Alexander, Cheol S. Eun, and S. Janakiramanan, "Asset Pricing and Dual Listing on Foreign Capital Markets: A Note," *Journal of Finance* (March 1987): 151–58.

3. Robert C. Merton, "A Simple Model of Capital Market Equilibrium with Incomplete Information," *Journal of Finance* (July 1987): 483–510.

4. This example was supplied by Grant Kvalheim of Merrill Lynch, whose help is greatly appreciated. The actual interest and exchange rates have been disguised.

5. This explanation is provided in Clifford W. Smith, Jr., Charles W. Smithson, and Lee M. Wakeman, "The Evolving Market for Swaps," *Midland Corporate Finance Journal* (Winter 1986): 20–32.

Chapter 6: Designing a Global Financing Strategy

1. This section is based on Donald R. Lessard and Alan C. Shapiro, "Guidelines for Global Financing Choices," *Midland Corporate Finance Journal* (Winter 1983): 68–80.

2. This insight was first presented in Merton Miller, "Debt and Taxes," *Journal of Finance* (May 1977): 261–76.

3. Alan C. Shapiro, "The Impact of Taxation on the Currency-of-Denomination Decision for Long-Term Foreign Borrowing and Lending," *Journal of International Business Studies* (Spring/Summer 1984): 15–25.

4. This view is expressed in Bradford Cornell and Alan C. Shapiro, "Corporate Stakeholders and Corporate Finance," *Financial Management* (Spring 1987): 5–14.

5. See "Diversifying Sources of Financing," *Business International Money Report*, 23 September 1977.

6. This point is made in Michael Adler, "The Cost of Capital and Valuation of a Two-Country Firm," *Journal of Finance* (March 1974): 119–32; and elaborated on in Alan C. Shapiro, "Financial Structure and Cost of Capital in the Multinational Corporation," *Journal of Financial and Quantitative Analysis* (June 1978): 211–26.

7. Robert B. Stobaugh, "Financing Foreign Subsidiaries of U.S.-Controlled Multinational Enterprises," *Journal of International Business Studies* (Summer 1970): 43–64.

8. "Policies of MNCs on Debt/Equity Mix," *Business International Money Report*, 21 September 1979.

Bibliography

Adler, Michael. "The Cost of Capital and Valuation of a Two-Country Firm." *Journal of Finance* (March 1974): 119-32.

Alexander, Gordon, Cheol S. Eun, and S. Janakiramanan. "Asset Pricing and Dual Listing on Foreign Capital Markets: A Note." *Journal of Finance* (March 1987): 151-58.

Baldwin, Carliss. "Competing for Capital in a Global Environment." *Midland Corporate Finance Journal* (Spring 1987): 43-64.

Bradley, David. "Managing Against Expropriation." *Harvard Business Review* (July-August 1977): 75-83.

Caves, Richard E. "International Corporations: The Industrial Economics of Foreign Investment." *Economica* (February 1971): 1-27.

Cornell, Bradford. "Spot Rates, Forward Rates, and Market Efficiency." *Journal of Financial Economics* 5 (1977): 55-65.

Cornell, Bradford, and Alan C. Shapiro. "Managing Foreign Exchange Risks." *Midland Corporate Finance Journal* (Fall 1983): 16-31.

_____. "Corporate Stakeholders and Corporate Finance," *Financial Management* (Spring 1987): 5-14.

Dufey, Gunter, and Sam L. Srinivasulu. "The Case for Corporate Management of Foreign Exchange Risk." *Financial Management* (Summer 1984): 54–62.

Dumas, Bernard. "The Theory of the Trading Firm Revisited." *Journal of Finance* (June 1978): 1014–29.

Fama, Eugene F. "Short-Term Interest Rates as Predictors of Inflation." *American Economic Review* (June 1975): 269–82.

Fatemi, Ali M. "Shareholder Benefits from Corporate International Diversification." *Journal of Finance* (December 1984): 1325–44.

Garner, C. Kent, and Alan C. Shapiro. "A Practical Method of Assessing Foreign Exchange Risk." *Midland Corporate Finance Journal* (Fall 1984): 6–17.

Giddy, Ian H. "The Foreign Exchange Options as a Hedging Tool," *Midland Corporate Finance Journal* (Fall 1983): 32–42.

Giddy, Ian H., and Gunter Dufey. "The Random Behavior of Flexible Exchange Rates." *Journal of International Business Studies* (Spring 1975): 1–32.

Goeltz, Richard Karl. "The Corporate Borrower and the International Capital Markets." Manuscript, March 6, 1984.

Hamel, Gary, and Prahalad, C.K. "Do You Really Have a Global Strategy?" *Harvard Business Review* (July-August 1985): 139–48.

Hodder, James E., and Lemma W. Senbet. "International Capital Structure Equilibrium." Working paper, January 1987.

Kester, W. Carl. "Today's Options for Tomorrow's Growth." *Harvard Business Review* (March-April 1984): 153–60.

Lessard, Donald R. "Evaluating Foreign Projects: An Adjusted Present Value Approach." In Donald R. Lessard, ed., *International Financial Management*. Boston: Warren, Gorham & Lamont, 1979.

_____. "Currency and Tax Considerations in International Financing." Teaching Note No. 3, MIT, Spring 1979.

_____. "Transfer Prices, Taxes, and Financial Markets: Implications of Internal Financial Transfers Within the Multinational Firm," in Robert G. Hawkins, ed. *The Economic Effects of Multinational Corporations*. Greenwich, Conn.: JAI Press, 1979.

_____. "World, Country, and Industry Relationships in Equity Returns: Implications for Risk Reduction Through International Diversification." *Financial Analysts Journal* (January-February 1976): 32–38.

_____. "Finance and Global Competition: Exploiting Financial Scope and Coping with Volatile Exchange Rates." *Midland Corporate Finance Journal* (Fall 1986): 6–29.

Lessard, Donald R., and John B. Lightstone. "Volatile Exchange Rates Can Put Operations at Risk." *Harvard Business Review* (July-August 1986): 107–14.

Lessard, Donald R., and Alan C. Shapiro. "Guidelines for Global Financing Choices." *Midland Corporate Finance Journal* (Winter 1983): 68–80.

Levich, Richard M. "Analyzing the Accuracy of Foreign Exchange Advisory Services: Theory and Evidence." In Richard Levich and Clas Wihlborg, eds., *Exchange Risk and Exposure*. Lexington, Mass.: D.C. Heath, 1980.

Mahajan, Arvind. "Pricing Risk of Expropriation." Working paper, 1988.

Merton, Robert C. "A Simple Model of Capital Market Equilibrium with Incomplete Information." *Journal of Finance* (July 1987): 483–510.

Officer, Lawrence H. "The Purchasing-Power-Parity Theory of Exchange Rates: A Review Article." *IMF Staff Papers* (March 1976): 1–60.

"Policies of MNCs on Debt/Equity Mix." *Business International Money Report*. 21 September 1979.

Robbins, Sidney M., and Robert B. Stobaugh. *Money in the Multinational Enterprise*. New York: Basic Books, 1973.

• Roll, Richard. "Violations of the Law of One Price and Their Implications for Differentially-Denominated Assets." In Marshall Sarnat and George Szego, eds., *International Finance and Trade*. Vol. 1. Cambridge, Mass.: Ballinger, 1979.

Rugman, Alan. "Risk Reduction by International Diversification." *Journal of International Business Studies* (Fall 1976): 75–80.

Rutenberg, David P. "Maneuvering Liquid Assets in a Multinational Company." *Management Science* (June 1970): B-671–84.

Shapiro, Alan C. "Capital Budgeting for the Multinational Corporation." *Financial Management* (Spring 1978): 7–16.

_____. "Currency Risk and Relative Price Risk." *Journal of Financial and Quantitative Analysis* (December 1984): 365–73.

_____. "Financial Structure and Cost of Capital in the Multinational Corporation." *Journal of Financial and Quantitative Analysis* (June 1978): 211–26.

_____. "The Impact of Taxation on the Currency-of-Denomination Decision for Long-Term Foreign Borrowing and Lending." *Journal of International Business Studies* (Spring/Summer 1984): 15–25.

_____. "Evaluating Financing Costs for Multinational Subsidiaries." *Journal of International Business Studies* (Fall 1975): 25–32.

_____. "Managing Against Currency Controls." Working paper, University of Southern California, 1980.

_____. "Managing Political Risk: A Policy Approach." *Columbia Journal of World Business* (Fall 1981): 63–70.

_____. *Multinational Financial Management*, 2nd edition. Boston: Allyn and Bacon, 1986.

_____. "What Does Purchasing Power Parity Mean?" *Journal of International Money and Finance* (December 1983): 295–318.

Shapiro, Alan C., and Titman, Sheridan. "An Integrated Approach to Corporate Risk Management." *Midland Corporate Finance Journal* (Summer 1985): 41–56.

Smith, Clifford W., Jr.; Charles W. Smithson; and Lee M. Wakeman. "The Evolving Market for Swaps," *Midland Corporate Finance Journal* (Winter 1986): 20–32.

Solnik, Bruno. "Why Not Diversify Internationally Rather Than Domestically?" *Financial Analysts Journal* (July-August 1974): 48–54.

Statement of Financial Accounting Standards No. 52. Stamford, Conn.: Financial Accounting Standards Board, December 1981.

Stobaugh, Robert B. "Financing Foreign Subsidiaries of U.S.-Controlled Multinational Enterprises." *Journal of International Business Studies* (Summer 1970): 43–64.

Stulz, Rene M. "A Model of International Asset Pricing." *Journal of Financial Economics* (December 1981): 383–406.

———. "Pricing Capital Assets in an International Setting: An Introduction." *Journal of International Business Studies* 15 (1985): 55–73.

Truitt, J. Frederick. "Expropriation of Foreign Investment: Summary of the Post-World War II Experience of American and British Investors in Less Developed Countries." *Journal of International Business Studies* (Fall 1970): 3–15

Vernon, Raymond. *Sovereignty at Bay.* New York: Basic Books, 1971.

Index

A

Accounting methods
  competition and, 80
  financial executive's role in, 5-6
  foreign exchange risk measurement
    and, 23, 24-25, 177-178
Accounts receivable
  cash management and, 72, 77-80
  credit extension and, 78-80
  credit management and, 77
Adjusted present value (APV),
    100-102
Advance purchasing, and inventory
  management, 81
Alexander, Gordon, 139
All-equity rate, 101
Arbitrage
  competitive market relationships
    with, 13-17
  definition of, 2
  Eurobonds and, 144
  fund flows and opportunities for,
    90-91
  risk and, 2-3
  tax, 2
Arbitrage pricing theory (APT), 3-4
Asset market model, in currency
  forecasting, 20-21
Association of International Bond
  Dealers, 142
Automobile manufacturing industry
  government subsidies and, 167
  overseas production facilities in, 8

pricing strategy and exchange
  risk in, 55
political risk and, 111
production facilities in, 61
product strategy in, 58

B

Back-to-back loans, and fund flows,
  93, 94-95
Balance of payments
  exchange rate and, 21, 22
  political risk and, 112
Banking systems
  cash movements and, 73-74
  currency controls and fund flows
    and, 94
  Eurocurrency market and,
    140-142
  international financial markets
    and, 138
  revolving underwriting facility
    (RUF) and, 149
  securitization and, 134-135
  swaps and, 159-161
  trends in corporate financing
    and, 132, 134-135
Bardepot, 70
Bearer bonds, in global financial
  strategy, 165-166
Beneficial Corporation, 131
Bonds
  breakdown by market of issue of,
    137, 138

international financial markets
for, 137
trends in corporate financing
and, 132
see also Eurobonds
Borrowing, *see* Loans
Brazil
debt swaps and, 159
foreign exchange risk and, 30
Bretton Woods system, and
currency forecasting, 18
British Telecommunications, 131,
140
Budgeting, and cash management,
71–72

C

Call option
government expropriation as,
113–114
hedging and, 44
Capital asset pricing, 3–4
Capital asset pricing model
(CAPM), 3–4, 102, 116–117
Capital budgeting, 99–111
adjusted present value (APV)
approach to, 100–102
adjustment of expected values in,
109–110
alternative frameworks for,
99–102
differences between domestic and
international firms in, 99
discount rate adjustment in, 109
estimates of incremental project
cash flows in, 103–104
exchange rate changes and
inflation and, 110–111
financial executive's role in
decisions on, 6
foreign investment strategy with,
124
growth options and, 106–108
issues in, 102–106
parent versus project cash flows
in, 102–103
payback period adjustment in,
109
political and economic risk
analysis with, 108–110

standard net present value (NPV)
approach to, 100
tax flows in, 104–106
Capital controls, and cash
management, 70
Capital costs, and foreign
investments, 116–123
Capital flight, and political risk, 112
Capital gains rate, and hedging
decision, 49
Capital markets
multinational corporation (MNC)
and segmented, 1
Capital shift, and competitive
market relationships, 16
Cash flows
budgeting and, 71
exchange rate changes and, 111
financial executive's role in
decisions on, 5–6
foreign exchange risk
measurement and, 24, 34
foreign investment analysis issues
with, 102–104, 106–108
growth options and, 106–108
hedging and, 38, 66
incremental project estimates of,
103–104
interest rate/currency swap and,
155
licensing and, 10
parent versus project, 102–103
political risk and, 115
risk and, 4
tax factors in, 105
Cash management, 69–77
cash planning and budgeting
and, 71–72
collection and disbursement in,
72–74
differences between domestic and
international, 70
government control and, 70
investment of excess funds in,
76–77
key areas of, 70
netting interaffiliate payments in,
74–75
objectives of, 69–70
optimal worldwide cash levels
and, 75–76
organization of, 70–71

reporting in, 72
Cash pooling, 75–76
Caterpillar Tractor, 59, 61, 140
Caves, Richard, 125
Centralization of cash management,
  70–71
Change, and global manager, 11
Chile
  debt swaps and, 159–160
  expropriation policy of, 170, 171
  foreign exchange risk and, 30
Citicorp, 138
Collection of funds, in cash
  management, 72–74
Competition
  credit extensions policies and, 80
  exchange rate management and, 50
  financial market globalization
    and, 136
  foreign exchange risk and relative
    price changes and, 28
  foreign investment strategy and,
    126, 128, 129–130
  global financing strategy and, 171
  hedging decisions and, 45
  key equilibrium relationships in,
    13–17
  licensing and, 10
  multinationalization of firms and,
    6–7
  pricing strategy and exchange
    risk in, 55
  production management and, 61,
    63, 64
Computers, and global financial
  marketplace, 5, 135
Contracts
  foreign exchange risk and, 27–28
  hedging risk sharing with, 41–42
Controls, *see* Currency controls;
  Exchange controls
Corporate financial, *see* Domestic
  corporate finance; International
  corporate finance
Corporation, *see* Domestic
  corporation; Multinational
  corporation (MNC)
Costs
  cash management and, 72, 74
  dividends in fund flows and, 96

Eurobonds and Eurocurrency
  comparison for, 147–148
  foreign investment capital and,
    116–123
  inventory stockpiling and, 81
  leading and lagging in fund flows
    and, 93
  production management and, 61, 62
  promotional strategy and, 57
  securitization and, 135
  short-term financing and, 84–87
  total risk and, 4
Credit extension
  accounts receivable and, 78–80
  competition and, 80
  example of, 79–80
Credit management, and accounts
  receivable, 77
Credit policy
  accounts receivable and, 78–80
  fund flows and, 90–91
  global financing strategy and,
    171, 172
Credit sales, and hedging, 40
Credit transfer, in cash
  management, 74
Cross Company, 167
Cruzado, foreign exchange risk and
  changes in, 30
Currency changes
  foreign exchange risk and, 28–30
  global financing strategy and, 164
  hedging and options in, 42–46
  illustration of, 30
  risk shifting and, 38–39
  short-term financing and, 85–87
  see also Devaluation; Revaluation
Currency controls
  dividends and, 95, 97
  expropriation and, 114
  loans in fund flows and, 94
  political risk and, 111, 120
Currency depreciation, and
  inflation, 15–16
Currency forecasting, 18–23, 34
  market-based, 19–22
  model evaluation in, 22–23
  requirements for successful, 18
  success of, 22–23
Currency swap
  fund flows and, 93, 95
  global financial strategy with, 153

D

Debit transfer, in cash
management, 74
Debt
fund flows and, 97–98
swaps and, 159–161
Development banks, 168
Delivery time, and production
management, 64
Depreciation of currency
cash flows and, 114
inflation and, 15–16
production facilities and, 61
Deutsche mark (DM)
hedging example with, 35, 36–37,
37–38, 39, 40, 41–42, 43–44
liability management and, 66
pricing strategy and exchange
risk in, 55
swaps and, 158
Devaluation
advance inventory purchases
and, 81
credit extension and, 78
foreign exchange risk and relative
price changes and, 29
hedging and, 47, 48
market segmentation and effects
of, 52
plant location and, 62
pricing strategy and, 53, 55, 56
product strategy and, 58
promotional strategy and, 57
Developing countries, market
expansion into, 9
Direct debiting, in cash movement,
74
Discount rate, in foreign investment
analysis, 109, 117–120, 121
Distribution system, and exchange
risk and, 55
Diversifiable risk, 4
Diversification
capital asset pricing model
(CAPM) and, 116
foreign investment and, 117–120
global financing strategy and, 172
stock market research on, 122–123
Dividends
currency controls and, 97
expropriation and, 114
fund flows and, 95–97

payout ratio for, 97
tax rates and, 96
variables affecting, 95
Dollar
Eurobonds and weakness of,
144
foreign exchange risk and relative
price changes and, 29
risk shifting and, 38–39
Domestic corporation
capital budgeting techniques of,
99
factors affecting, 1
Domestic corporate finance
behavioral definition of
multinational corporation and, 10
capital asset pricing and, 3–4
capital budgeting in, 99
cash management in, 70
efficient financial market and, 3
financial executive role in, 5–6
international domestic finance
and, 1, 2–6, 177
risk arbitrage and, 2–3
total risk and, 4
working capital management in,
69
Drawdown, in Eurocurrency
market, 142, 151
Dual Syndicate equity offerings,
140
Dufey, Gunter, 49

E

Eastman Kodak, 154–158, 160
Economic analysis
domestic financial management
and, 2
foreign exchange risk
measurement and, 23, 24–25
foreign investment analysis and,
108–110, 124, 179
Economic conditions, and exchange
rate changes, 25–26
Economic exposure, and foreign
exchange risk, 23, 25–26, 31
Economies of scale
foreign investment strategy and,
127, 128
pricing strategy and exchange
risk and, 54

production management and, 61
Efficient financial market, *see*
Market efficiency
Employee motivation, and
production costs, 62
Entry strategy, for foreign markets,
9, 130
Equity, and fund flows, 97–98
Equity market, in international
finance, 139–140
Eun, Cheol, 139
Eurobonds, 142–146
advantages of, 145
diversification with, 172
Eurocurrency compared with,
147–149
floating-rate note (FRN) and,
144–145
growth in use of, 142–143
note issuance facility (NIF)
compared with, 151–152
secondary market for, 146–147
swaps in, 152
weakness of dollar and, 144
Eurocurrency market
Eurobonds compared with,
147–149
international finance and, 140–142
Euroequity issues, 140
Euronotes, in note issuance facility
(NIF), 150
European Currency Unit (ECU),
145–146
Evaluation criteria, in foreign
investment analysis, 128–129
Exchange controls
foreign investment analysis issues
and, 102
fund flows and, 90, 91, 92, 95
multinational corporation (MNC)
and, 1
Exchange rate
adjustment time following
changes in, 64–65
balance of payments and, 21, 22
competitive market relationships
with, 14, 15, 16
currency forecasting and, 20–21
domestic inflation and, 15–16
economic analysis and, 2

foreign investment analysis and,
110–111
government involvement in, 51
hedging decisions and changes
in, 49
multinational corporation (MNC)
and changes in, 1
neutrality of money in, 15
risk in, *see* Foreign exchange risk
short-term financing and, 82–83
Exchange risk, *see* Foreign
exchange risk
Executives
efficient market and role of, 5–6
financial management of
exchange risk and, 66–67
impact of decisions of, 6
Expansion into foreign markets
acquisition of affiliates for, 11
behavioral definition of
multinational corporation and, 10
change and, 11
creating own affiliates for, 9
entry strategy into, 9
exporting and, 7–8
global manager and, 11
licensing and, 9–10
multinationalization of firms and,
6–7
overseas production and, 8–9
phases of, 7
strategies for, 7
total risk and, 4
Export-Import Bank (Ex-Im Bank), 167
Exporting
expansion into foreign markets
and, 7–8
foreign exchange risk and relative
price changes and, 29
foreign investment strategy and,
129
marketing management of exchange
risk and, 53
production management and, 60
product strategy in, 58
promotional strategy and, 57
Expropriation, 1
calculation of probability of, 115
defensive ploy for, 114
global financing strategy and,
170, 171
political risk and, 111, 113–114, 115

F

Fatemi, Ali, 122
Federal government, *see* Government policy
Federal Reserve Board, 172
Fees, and fund flows, 92–93
Financial management, *see* Domestic corporate finance; International corporate finance
Financial markets, 136–140
  banking market and, 138
  bond market and, 137
  currency forecasting based on, 19–22
  deregulation of, 135
  economic analysis of, 2
  equity market in, 139–140
  foreign access to, 137
  international financing and, 131–140
  political stability and, 136
  securitization and, 134–135
Financial strategy, 163–175, 180
  access to funds and, 171–173
  after-tax financing costs minimization in, 164–168
  bearer bonds in, 165–166
  currency choice in, 164
  debt versus equity financing in, 166
  development banks and, 168
  diversification and, 172
  excess borrowing and, 172–173
  exchange risk and, 169
  government credit and capital controls and, 166–167
  government subsidies and incentives and, 167–168
  objectives of, 163
  operating risk reduction in, 168–173
  political risk and, 169–170
  product market risk and, 170–171
  worldwide financial structure and, 173–175
  zero-coupon bonds in, 165
Financing foreign operations, 131–161
  banking market in, 138
  bond market in, 137, 138
  equity market in, 139–140
  Eurobonds in, 142–146, 147–149, 151–152
  Eurocurrency market in, 140–142, 147–149
  financial intermediaries in, 134–136
  foreign access to domestic markets in, 137
  international financial markets in, 136–140
  nation trends in, 132–134
  note issuance facility (NIF) in, 149–152
  secondary market in, 146–147
  swaps in, 152–161
First-in, first-out method (FIFO) method, 6
Fisher effect (FE)
  competitive market relationships with, 14, 15, 16, 177
  technical description of, 17
Fixed-rate debt, and foreign exchange risk, 27
Flexible manufacturing systems, 63–64
Float, and cash management, 72
Floating-rate note (FRN), 144–145, 152
Floating rate system, and currency forecasting, 18
Ford Motor Company, 55, 61, 167
Forecasting
  currency, *see* Currency forecasting
  excess funds investment and, 76
  hedging decision and, 34
  success of services in, 22–23
Foreign Credit Restraint Program, 138
Foreign exchange rate, *see* Exchange rate
Foreign exchange risk
  adjustment period following exchange rate change and, 64–65
  "balance sheet" approach to, 23, 178
  contracts and, 27–28
  currency forecasting in, 18–23
  definition of, 23, 24
  dividends in fund flows and, 95
  domestic cost cutting and, 62
  economic consequences of exchange rate changes and, 25–26
  economic versus accounting values in, 24–25
  financial management of, 65–67

Fisher effect (FE) and, 15, 16
forecasting of, 34
forward rate as unbiased predictor
    of future spot rate and, 17
global financing strategy and, 169
government involvement in
    currency change and, 51
hedging decision and, 33–49
illustration and, 27
inflation and currency depreciation
    and, 15–16
inflation and exchange risk and,
    26–28, 178
input mix in, 59–60
interest rate parity (IRP) and, 16–17
international Fisher effect (IFE) and,
    15, 16
key equilibrium relationships in,
    13–17
liability management in, 65–66
management of, 49–67
manager's role in, 66–67
market selection in, 52–53
measurement of risk in, 23–33
multinational corporation (MNC)
    and, 27
multiperiod exposure in, 32
nominal interest rate in, 16
operational measure of exchange
    risk in, 31–33
planning and, 62–65
pricing strategy in, 53–56
production management in, 59–65
product strategy in, 57–59
promotional strategy in, 57
purchasing power parity (PPP) and,
    15, 16
relative price changes and, 28–30,
    33–34
short-term financing and, 83, 84–85
swaps and, 158–159
time length of real change in, 50–51
Foreign investment analysis, 99–130,
179
adjusted present value (APV)
    approach in, 100–102
capital budgeting in, 99–111, 124
capital markets and, 121–122
cash flow adjustments for political
    risk in, 115

competitive advantages in, 126,
    129–130
cost of capital for, 116–123
discount rates in, 109, 117–120
economic analysis in, 2
estimates of incremental project
    cash flows in, 103–104
evaluation criteria in, 128–129
exchange rate changes and inflation
    in, 110–111
expected values adjustment in,
    109–110
growth options in, 106–108
issues in, 102–106
less developed countries (LDCs)
    and, 118–119
licensing and, 9–10
market imperfection and, 125
net present value (NPV) approach
    in, 100, 123–124
organizational skills and, 125–126
parent versus project cash flows in,
    102–103
payback period adjustment in, 109
policies on, 126–130
political and economic risk analysis
    in, 108–110, 179
political risk management in,
    114–115
political risk measurement in,
    112–114
portfolio diversification and,
    117–120
product development and, 127
project beta estimates in, 121–122
stock market research on, 122–123
strategy for, 123–130, 180
systematic risk of project in, 119–120
tax factors in, 104–106
total risk reduction and, 123
Foreign market expansion, *see*
Expansion into foreign markets
Foreign tax credit (FTC)
dividends and, 96
global financing strategy and, 174
Forward contract
hedging and, 42, 45–46, 49
inventory management with, 81
short-term financing and, 82–83
Forward market hedge, 35–37, 38, 40

Forward rates
  competitive market relationships
    with, 14
  currency forecasting and, 19
  interest rate parity (IRP) and, 16–17
  as unbiased predictor of future spot
    rate (UFR), 14, 17
Franchise, and foreign investment,
  127
Fronting loans, and fund flows, 94
Fundamental analysis, in currency
  forecasting, 20–21
Fund flows
  advantages of, 87
  arbitrage opportunities in, 90–91
  credit restraint or controls in, 90–91
  debt versus equity in, 97–98
  dividends and, 95–97
  fees and royalties and, 92–93
  financial linkage possibilities in, 88,
    89
  intracorporate loans and, 88, 93–95
  leading and lagging and, 93
  management of, 87–98
  mechanisms for, 91–98
  mode of transfer in, 88
  multinational financial system and,
    88–90
  time flexibility and, 88–90
  transfer pricing in, 91–92

G

General Motors, 55, 61, 131
Germany, *see* West Germany
Government policy
  capital controls ad, 166–167
  cash management and, 70
  currency changes and foreign
    exchange risk and, 29
  currency controls and, 94, 95
  currency forecasting and, 18
  exchange rate management and, 51
  expropriation targets in, 113–114
  financial market deregulation
    by, 135
  fund flows and, 90–91
  global financial marketplace
    and, 5, 166–168
  hedging decisions and, 48
  international financial markets
    and, 136, 138

  political risk and, 111–115
  price controls and, 56
  subsidies and incentives in,
    167–168
Growth options, and foreign
  investment
  analysis issues, 106–108

H

Hedging, 33–49
  contracts in, 42, 45–46
  currency risk sharing in, 41–42
  exposure netting in, 40–41
  foreign currency options in, 42–46
  forecast of exchange risk and, 34
  forward market, 35–37
  illustration used in, 35, 36–37,
    37–38, 39, 40, 41–42, 43–44, 66
  local government and, 48
  money market, 37–38
  objectives of, 49
  portfolio approach to, 40–41
  pricing decisions and, 39–40
  residual exposure in, 34–35
  risk shifting in, 38–39
  sources of risk and, 33
  techniques for, 34–35, 47, 48
  total risk and, 4
  value of, 46–49

I

ICI, 129
Imports
  advance inventory purchases
    and, 81
  currency changes and, 30
  government subsidies and,
    167–168
  pricing strategy and exchange
    risk in, 55
Incentives, in government financial
  policy, 167–168
Inflation
  advance inventory purchases
    and, 81
  competitive market relationships
    with, 15
  credit extension and, 77
  currency depreciation and, 15–16
  currency forecasting and, 20
  exchange risk and, 26–28, 178

foreign investment analysis and, 110–111
last-in, first-out (LIFO) method and, 5
multinational corporation (MNC) and varying rates of, 1
plant location and, 62
purchasing power parity (PPP) and, 16
Innovation
pricing strategy and, 54
product strategy and, 59
Input mix, in production, 59–60
Inter-American Development Bank, 168
Interest Equalization Tax (IET), 137
Interest rate/currency swap, 153, 154–158
Interest rate parity (IRP)
competitive market relationships with, 14, 16–17
technical description of, 17
Interest rates
cash management and, 71
competitive market relationships with, 15
currency forecasting and, 19
Eurobonds and, 143
growth potential and, 107
loans in fund flows and, 97–98
Interest rate swap, 153
Internal Revenue Code, and fund flows, 92
Internal Revenue Service, and tax credits for dividends, 96
International cash management, *see* Cash management
International corporate finance
behavioral definition of multi-national corporation and, 10
capital asset pricing and, 3–4
domestic corporate finance and, 1, 2–6, 177
economic analysis applied to, 2
efficient financial market and, 3
financial executive's role in decisions on, 5–6
international domestic finance and, 1, 2–6
risk arbitrage and, 2–3
total risk and, 4

International financial markets, *see* Financial markets
International Fisher effect (IFE)
competitive market relationships with, 14, 15, 16, 177
foreign exchange risk measurement and, 24–25
short-term financing and, 82
technical description of, 17
Internationalization of firms, *see* Expansion into foreign markets
Inventory management, 80–82
advance purchases in, 81
difficulties with, 80–81
stockpiling in, 81–82
Investment
cash management of excess funds with, 76–77
loans in fund flows and, 97–98
see also Foreign investment analysis
Investment flows, 88

J

Janakiramanan, S., 139
Japanese companies
exchange rate change adjustments by, 64, 65
financing patterns of, 134
foreign exchange risk and relative price changes and, 28
foreign investment strategy of, 128
international financial markets and, 136, 137, 138
political risk and, 111
pricing strategy and exchange risk in, 55
zero-coupon bonds ad, 165
JVC, 65

K

Kennecott, 170, 171
Kester, W. Carl, 108
Kollmorgen Corporation, 59

L

Labor contracts, and foreign exchange risk, 27
Labor costs, and foreign investment, 128

Last-in, first-out (LIFO) method,
5–6
Latin America
debt swaps in, 160
political risk in, 112–113
Law of one price, 13, 26–27
Leading and lagging, and fund
flows, 88, 93
Leases, and foreign exchange risk,
27
Lessard, Donald, 88, 110, 117
Less developed countries (LDCs)
debt swaps and, 159
political risks of foreign
investment in, 118–119
Levish, Richard, 23
Liability management, and exchange
risk, 65–66
Licensing, and expansion into
foreign markets, 9–10
Link financing, and fund flows, 94
Loans
Eurocurrency market margin
with, 141
excess borrowing with, 172–173
fund flows with, 88, 93–95, 97–98
hedging decisions and, 34, 47, 48
swaps with, 159–161
trends in corporate financing and,
132, 134–135
types of, 93
see also Short-term financing
Local government, and hedging
decisions, 48
Location of plant, 62
Lock box, in cash movements, 73
London interbank offer rate
(LIBOR), 141

M

Machinery and Allied Products
Institute, 59
Mahajan, Arvind, 113
Management, *see* Domestic corporate
finance; Executives; Foreign
exchange risk; International
corporate finance
Manager
change and, 11

expansion into foreign markets
and, 11
financial management of exchange
risk and, 66–67
hedging decisions and, 49
Manufacturing
currency changes and, 30
see also Production
Margin, in Eurocurrency market,
141
Market efficiency
currency forecasting and, 22
definition of, 3
financial executive's role in, 5–6
foreign exchange risk
measurement and, 24
global nature of, 5
Marketing
exchange rate management and,
50, 52–59
market selection in, 52–53
pricing strategy in, 53–56
product deletion decision in, 58
product strategy in, 57–59
promotional strategy in, 57
Market risk, 4
Markets
entry strategy for, 9
expansion into, *see* Expansion
into foreign markets
financial, *see* Financial markets
foreign investment strategy and,
129
global financing strategy and,
170–171
selection of, in exchange risk
management, 52–53
Market segmentation, and exchange
risk management, 52–53
Matsushita, 128
Maxwell House, 60
Merrill Lynch, 154–158
Merton, Robert, 139
Mexico, 47
debt swaps and, 159, 160–161
exchange rate management and,
51
foreign exchange risk and
devaluation in, 29
plant location and, 62
pricing strategy and exchange risk
in, 55

Michelin, 9
MNC, *see* Multinational corporation (MNC)
Mobilization points, in cash movements, 73
Models
currency forecasting, 18, 19–23
political risk and, 112–113
Money markets
hedging and, 37–38
international financial access to, 137
multinational corporation (MNC) and multiple, 1
Money supply
competitive market relationships with, 15
currency forecasting and, 20
Motivation of employees, and production costs, 62
Multinational corporation (MNC)
advantages of, 1
expansion into foreign markets and behavioral definition of, 11
factors affecting, 1
foreign exchange risk and, 27–28, 29
growth options for, 106
need to internationalize tools of domestic financial analysis for, 1
Multinationalization of firms, 6–7

N

National income growth rates, and currency forecasting, 20
Nationalization, 1
Natomas, 172
Net present value (NPV)
capital budgeting and, 100
foreign investment strategy and, 123–124
growth potential and, 107
Netherlands, and international financial markets, 137
Netting system, in cash management, 74–75
New product development
foreign investment strategy and, 127
pricing strategy and exchange risk and, 56

production management and, 61
strategy for, 57–58
Nominal interest rate
competitive market relationships and, 16
exchange rate changes and, 26
short-term financing and, 82–83
Note issuance facility (NIF)
Eurobonds compared with, 151–152
operation of, 149–152

O

Office of Foreign Direct Investment (OFDI), 70, 166
Operational measure of exchange risk, 31–33
calculation of, 31–32
limitations of, 33
multiperiod exposure in, 32
Organization for Economic Cooperation and Development, 138
Organizational skills, and foreign investment, 125–126
Overseas expansion, *see* Expansion into foreign markets

P

Parallel loan, and fund flows, 93, 94
Patents, and fund flows, 92
Payback period, in foreign investment analysis, 109
Payments netting, in cash management, 74–75
Payments schedule, in fund flows, 88–90
Payout ratio, for dividends, 97
Penetration pricing, and exchange risk, 54
Peso (Chile)
debt swaps and, 159–160
foreign exchange risk and, 30
Peso (Mexico)
debt swaps and, 159, 160–161
exchange rate management and, 51
foreign exchange risk and devaluation in, 29
hedging decisions and, 47
pricing strategy and exchange risk in, 55

Planning
 cash management and, 71-72
 production management and,
  62–65
Plants
 foreign location of, 63–64
 shifting production among, 60–61
Pools, in cash management, 75–76
Political risk
 capital flight and, 112
 cash flow adjustments for, 115
 differences in susceptibilities to,
  113
 foreign investment analysis and,
  108–110, 111–115, 179
 global financing strategy and,
  169–170
 government expropriation and,
  113–114
 international financial markets
  and, 136
 management of, 114–115
 measurement of, 112–114
 models of, 112–113
 multinational corporation (MNC)
  and, 1
 short-term financing and, 83–84
Pollution control regulation, 111
Portfolio analysis
 advance inventory purchases
  and, 81
 capital asset pricing and, 4
 excess funds investment and,
  76–77
 foreign investment risk and,
  117–120, 121
 hedging and, 40–41
 project beta estimates in, 121–122
 stock market research on, 122–123
Price
 arbitrage and, 2
 competitive market relationships
  with, 14–15
 devaluation and, 55
 discount rate for foreign projects
  and, 117
 exchange rate changes and, 16,
  28–30, 33–34
 future sales and, 55–56
 government controls over, 56
 hedging and, 33–34, 39–40, 45

market efficiency and, 3
marketing management of
 exchange risk and strategy in,
  53–56
risk shifting and currency choices
 and, 38–39
systematic risk and, 4
Price skimming, and exchange
 risk, 54
Production
 adjustment period after exchange
  rate change in, 64–65
 areas covered by, 8–9
 competitive position and, 63, 64
 domestic cost cutting in, 62
 exchange rate volatility and, 63
 exchange risk management and,
  50, 59–65
 expansion into foreign markets
  and, 8–9
 flexible systems in, 63–64
 input mix in, 59–60
 licensing and, 9–10
 planning in, 62–65
 plant location in, 62
 product delivery time in, 64
 shifting plants in, 60–61
Productivity, and production costs,
 62
Products
 delivery time for, 64
 deletion decision for, 58
 foreign investment strategy and,
  127
 global financing strategy and,
  170–171
 innovation in, 59
 line decisions for, 58
 marketing management of
  exchange risk and strategy for,
   57–59
 multinationalization of firms and,
  6–7
 see also New product development
Profit
 hedging decisions and, 45
 foreign investment strategy and,
  126–128
 production facilities and, 61
Projections, *see* Forecasting
Promotional strategy, in marketing
 management of exchange risk, 57

Purchasing policies, and inventory management, 81
Purchasing power parity (PPP)
  competitive market relationships with, 14, 15, 16, 177
  foreign exchange risk measurement and, 24–25, 26, 51
  technical description of, 17
Put option, and hedging, 44–46

Q

Quality of product, and costs, 62

R

Real exchange rate, and economic exposure, 25–26
Real interest rate, in competitive market relationships, 16
Real operating exposure, and exchange rate changes, 25
Relative price changes, and exchange rate changes, 26, 28–30
Rent, and foreign exchange risk, 27
Reporting, in cash management, 72
Research and development (R&D), and foreign investment strategy, 127, 128
Returns
  capital asset pricing and, 3–4
  foreign investment strategy and, 126–128
  risk arbitrage and, 2–3
Revaluation, and liability management, 66
Revolving underwriting facility (RUF), and Eurobonds, 149
Risk
  capital asset pricing and, 3–4
  cash flows and, 4
  economic analysis of measurement and pricing of, 2
  foreign exchange and, *see* Foreign exchange risk
  foreign investments and reduction of, 123
  global financing strategy and, 168–173, 180
  growth potential and, 107
  hedging and sources of, 33
  shifting of, 38

short-term financing and, 84–85
systematic or market, 4
total, 4
unsystematic or diversifiable, 4
Risk arbitrage, 2–3
Robbins, Sidney, 92
Royalties, and fund flows, 92–93
Rutenberg, David, 88

S

Sales
  credit extension and, 77, 78
  hedging and, 40
  pricing strategy and exchange risk in, 55–56
  total risk and, 4
Scale exonomies, *see* Economies of scale
Secondary market, and Eurobonds, 146–147
Securitization, and financial markets, 134–135
Shapiro, Alan C., 7, 48
Shareholders, and foreign exchange risk, 24
Short-term note issuance facilities (SNIFs), 149
Short-term financing, 82–87
  cost calculation in, 85–87
  key factors in, 82–84
  objectives in, 84–85
SKE, 8
Ski industry, 57
Solnik, Bruno, 117
Sony, 128
Spot rates
  forward rate as unbiased predictor of (UFR), 14, 17
  hedging and, 40
  interest rate parity (IRP) and, 17
Standard net present value (NPV), 100
Stobaugh, Robert, 92, 174
Stock issues, and international equity market, 139–140
Stockpiling, in inventory management, 81–82
Strategies
  exchange rate management with, 50, 52

expansion into foreign markets
with, 7
financial, *see* Financial strategy
foreign investments and, 123–130,
180
product management of exchange
risk with, 59
Subpart F income, 96
Subsidies, in government financial
policy, 167–168
Swaps
advantages of, 158–159
bank loan, 159–161
fund flows and, 93, 95
illustration of, 154–158
international finance with, 152–161
types of, 153
Swiss Bank Corporation, 131, 172
Swiss franc
Eurobonds and use of, 145
relative price changes with, 28
Switzerland, and international
financial markets, 136, 137
Systematic risk, 4

T

Tariffs, and fund flows, 91, 92
Tax arbitrage, 2
Eurobonds and, 144
fund flows and opportunities for,
90
global financing strategy and,
164–166
Tax credits
dividends and, 95
global financing strategy and, 174
Tax management
bearer bonds ad, 166
financial executive's role in
decisions on, 6
fund flows and, 91, 98
global financing strategy and,
164–166, 175, 180
Tax Reform Act, 175
Tax systems
arbitrage and, 2
dividends and fund flows and, 96
Eurobonds and, 144
foreign investment analysis and,
102, 104–106, 120
hedging decisions and, 49

international financial markets
and, 137
multinational corporation (MNC)
and differences among national,
1
political risk and, 111
short-term financing and, 83–84
tax credits for dividends in, 96
Technical analysis, in currency
forecasting, 21–22
Technology, and pricing strategy, 54
Telecommunications, and global
financial marketplace, 5, 135
Time factors
cash management and, 72–73
Euronote market and, 152
exchange rate management and
change persistence and, 50–51
fund flows and, 88–90
growth potential and, 107
product strategy and, 57–58
Tire manufacturing industry, 9
Top management, *see* Executives
Total risk
effects of, 4
foreign investments and reduction
of, 123
Trademarks, and fund flows, 92
Traditional flow model, in currency
forecasting, 20
Transaction costs, in cash
management, 72
Transaction operating exposure,
and exchange rate changes, 25
Transfer prices, and fund flows,
88, 91–92
Transfers of funds
cash management and, 73
fund flows and, 88
Transportation, and overseas
production, 8

U

Unions, and production costs, 62
Unsystematic risk, 4

V

Value compensation, in cash
management, 74
Vernon, Raymond, 54
Victor Company of Japan, 65
Volkswagen, 8, 58, 66

W

West Germany
  cash management and, 70
  financing patterns of, 132, 134
  hedging example with, 35, 36–37,
    37–38, 39, 40, 41–42, 43–44
  international financial markets
    and, 137, 140
  liability management and, 66
  pricing strategy and exchange
    risk and, 55
  swaps and, 158
Westinghouse Electric Corporation,
  60
Wire transfers, in cash
  management, 73
Working capital management, 69–98
  accounts receivable management
    in, 77–80
  cash management in, 69–77, 377
  differences between domestic
    and international, 69
  financial executive's role in
    decisions on, 6
  intracorporate fund flows in, 87–98
  inventory management in, 80–82
  short-term financing in, 82–87
World Bank, 168

Y

Yen
  exchange rate change adjustment
    by, 64
  pricing strategy and exchange
    risk in, 55

Z

Zero-coupon bonds
  global financing strategy with, 165
  swaps and, 154–155

About the Author

Alan C. Shapiro is professor of finance and business economics at the School of Business Administration, University of Southern California. Previously, he was an assistant professor at the Wharton School of The University of Pennsylvania. He has also been a visiting professor at UCLA, the Stockholm School of Economics, the University of British Columbia, and the University of Hawaii. He received a B.A. in mathematics from Rice University and a Ph.D. in economics from Carnegie-Mellon University.

Dr. Shapiro's specialty is international financial management. He is currently researching the links between corporate finance and corporate strategy. He has engaged in consulting assignments with numerous companies and banks, and has been an expert witness in legal cases involving valuation, economic damages, transfer pricing, and takeovers. He has taught in numerous executive education programs; conducted in-house training programs in corporate finance and international finance and economics for banks, corporations, and law firms, and lectured worldwide on problems of international finance and economics.

Well known for his best-selling textbook, *Multinational Financial Management*, Dr. Shapiro has also published over forty articles in leading academic journals and two monographs. His newest textbook is entitled *Modern Corporate Finance*.